To. Robin

Heres to making your culinary dreams come true & making magic is your kitchen...

Thanks for all your work. Heres to changing school food is 2012

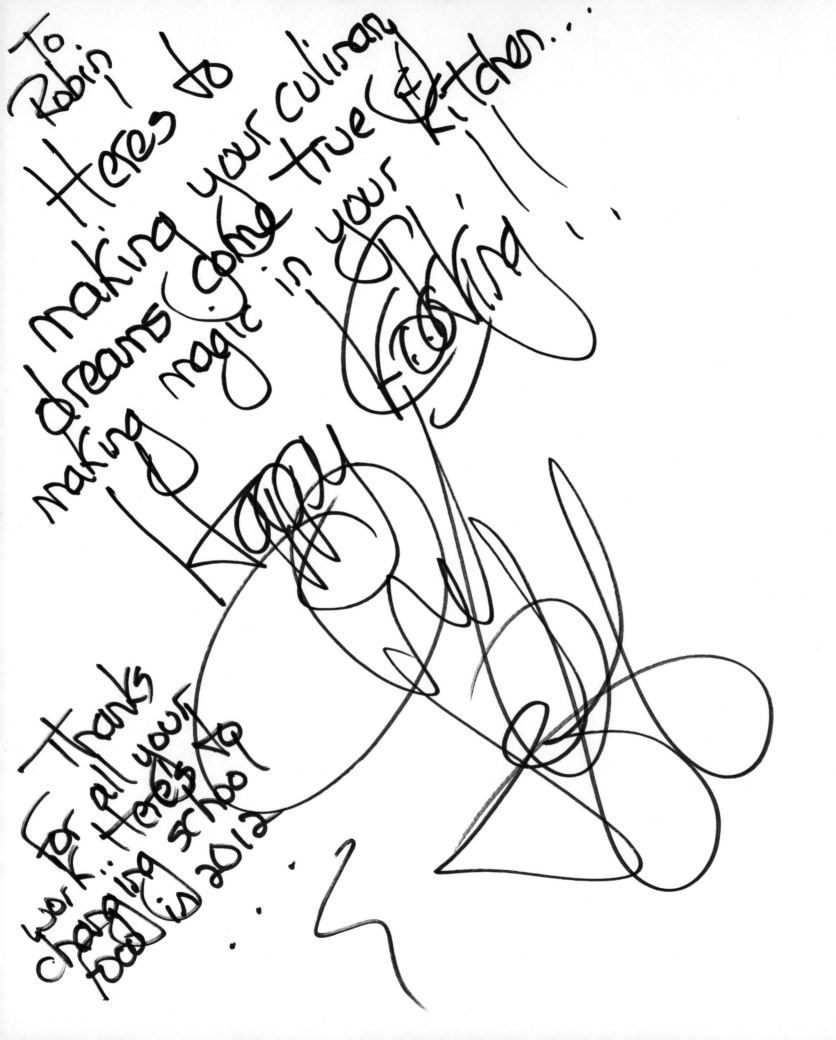

From Terra's Table

New American Food, Fresh From Southern California's Organic Farms

Jeff Rossman

PHOTOGRAPHY BY PAUL BODY

Chefs Press, Inc.

San Diego, California

From Terra's Table

New American Food, Fresh From Southern California's Organic Farms

Jeff Rossman

PHOTOGRAPHY BY PAUL BODY

Published by Chefs Press, Inc., San Diego, California
www.chefspress.com

Publisher: Amy Stirnkorb
President & CEO: Bruce Glassman
Executive Vice President: Michael D. Pawlenty
Photographs © Paul Body, Paul Body Photography,
www.paulbodyphoto.com
Consulting Editor: David Nelson
Proofreader: Bob Anderson
Maps: Paul Horn

Special thanks to:
Ryan Ross at Karl Strauss Brewery for all the delicious beer pairings he created for this book and for the Beer Advice column.
Jena Francis at Karl Strauss Brewery for her help in providing material for this book.
Andrea Peterson and Blue Heron Farm for letting us photograph our beautiful cover on their property.
Vernon Kindred at Fallbrook Winery for his review of the Wine Advice column.
Ira Gourvitz at Fallbrook Winery, Jim and Joe Hart at Hart Winery, Carolyn Bennett at Milagro Farm Winery, Crystal Magon and Dean Thomas at South Coast Winery, and Emily Eyre at Orfila Winery for their help with the winery profiles.
Terri Hughes-Oelrich at Albert Einstein Academies, Cindy Marten at Central Elementary School, Stan Miller at NCCS Gardening Program, Debbie Kornberg at San Diego Jewish Academy, AC "education" at Temecula Valley Slow Food and Hillcrest Academy, and Yvonne Campbell at San Pasqual Academy for their help with the school profiles.
Tina & David Barnes at Crows Pass Farm, Andrea Peterson at Blue Heron Farm, Jonathan Reinbold at Tierra Miguel Farm, Gail Cunningham at Cunningham Organic Farm, Robin at Suzie's and Sun Grown Farm, Phil Noble at Sage Mountain Farm, Noel Stehly at Stehly Farms Organics, and Sandra Broussard at Be Wise Ranch for their help with the farm profiles.

ISBN-13: 978-0-9816222-2-4
ISBN-10: 0-9816222-2-4

First Edition
Printed in China

Dedication

"To all the farmers that are at one with their dirt, to all the teachers, principals, parents and volunteers who work in the school gardens, and to all the chefs, groups, individuals, foundations, organizations, and educators helping us change school food, YOU ROCK!!"

Local, Organic, Sustainable, Grass- or Corn-Fed Beef ... Demystifying the Myth of Labeling

We all need to make conscious decisions!

You, the educated consumer, want to be informed and "do the right thing." You want to know where your food comes from, how it's grown, caught, handled, and processed. Many consumers know to look for "sustainable" and "organic" and "locally sourced" items, but a good deal of people are unsure about exactly what those labels mean. Furthermore, each category of food has its own specific terminology. Here's a brief overview of the main food categories and what the labels mean. Bottom line — ask your grocer, butcher, fishmonger, or other food-seller where he or she sources from. Make sure they buy from reputable organizations that participate in environmentally friendly, or "green," business practices.

Produce: Farmers' Markets certainly guarantee you "locally grown," but that's not always true at the grocery store. "Locally grown" can be a relative term — it can be misleading because some sources (grocery stores included) may use "local" to label anything that comes from your state, or even your region. For the San Diego Growers® and the San Diego Farm to School Initiative, "local" is defined as anything that comes from within 25 miles of the county line. With local produce, you know that you're not only supporting local or regional farmers, you're also getting food that hasn't been sitting in a truck forever, and has used a minimal amount of fossil fuel and other energy to reach you. It has been proven that foods grown in your backyard and eaten within days of harvest have more nutrients and cause fewer allergic reactions. Organic farming excludes or strictly limits the use of synthetic fertilizers and synthetic pesticides, plant-growth regulators, livestock antibiotics, food additives, and genetically modified organisms. Sustainable farms maximize the use of their own resources in the growing of their food, which means they minimize their impact on the environment by being relatively self-sufficient.

Fish: The Monterey Bay Aquarium's Seafood Watch® program evaluates the ecological sustainability of wild-caught and farmed seafood commonly found in the United States marketplace. Sustainable seafood originates from sources, whether wild-caught or farmed, that can maintain or increase production in a manner that doesn't jeopardize their ecosystem. There is a huge misconception that farmed fish is bad, but it's not a black-and-white issue. For some species, wild-caught fish is the most environmentally conscious choice; in other cases, farmed fish is better. There are various kinds of "wild-caught" fishing techniques, some of which are harmful to the marine environment (pursing or net catching) and some of which are not (troll or line catching). But even line-caught fish are problematic if it's a species that's threatened or endangered. There are also many criteria to judge a farm, but if they have a high water-to-fish ratio and use good environmental practices, they are generally considered a good source. The best way to sort it all out: go to www.montereybayaquarium.org and consult their most recent Seafood Watch® information.

Meat, Dairy, Poultry and Eggs: Organic feed must be used at all times for cattle and other meat animals. In addition, an ideal producer engages in humane practices, bars hormones and antibiotics, and allows the animals to be raised with proper shelter, sufficient space, and the ability to engage in natural behaviors. Many people debate whether grass-fed is better than corn-fed meat, but all agree that the animals should be raised as humanely as possible. When talking about poultry and eggs, "free range" or "cage free" indicates that the animals have not been raised in huge, crowded, "factory-style" pens and that they've been cared for in a more humane and environmentally friendly manner.

Acknowledgments

I tell everyone, "you're only as good as the people around you:" that's both personally and professionally. I wouldn't even be in this business if it weren't for my parents, Mike and Bobbi Rossman. They believed in me enough to invest in me and my restaurant concept to create Terra in the first place. They've also allowed me freedom to create, play, and leave to go on farm and school tours and helped pay for the food and time that went into the creation of this book.

Without my son, Aaron, I would've never had the passion and the drive to succeed and provide; it's funny what having a family does to you. Thanks, Aaron, for spending long days at the restaurant bouncing back and forth from learning in the kitchen to playing games on the office computer to watching TV at the bar.

To my partner and rock, Jody, for enduring those long hours of my writing and editing recipes at the restaurant and coming home late, sometimes even after you've gone to sleep. Thanks also to your shop Antiques at the Village in La Mesa for providing some amazing props and plates for the pictures in the book. I always brag about you and the fact that you are an amazing and incredible person for allowing me to do what I do. Thanks to Jody's son, John Michael, for not bugging me to play every night when I came home to work on my laptop after dinner. Max and Jake, our two dogs, were next to me on the couch for a countless number of hours while I was typing into the wee hours of the night: I hope I didn't neglect you guys too badly.

To my guys in the kitchen: Jorge, Enrique, Mario, David, Fernando, and especially Benito for standing behind me and keeping the restaurant going while I was on farm and school tours and spending tons of time in the office writing and editing.

To the Harrington Brothers and JR at Specialty Produce who were awesome in helping out with produce for the food shots.

This book might not be finished if it weren't for Lisa Gradillas, my assistant and director of operations. She kept me focused and the book on track while screening phone calls and working on a thousand other things when I wasn't available.

Paul Body, the brilliant San Diego food photographer, rose to the challenge of this project and truly knocked it out of the park.

To my publishers, Chefs Press, Amy Stirnkorb, Bruce Glassman, and Michael Pawlenty for believing in me and this important project. For the editing, graphics, and always having my back to steer this book in the proper direction.

This book certainly wouldn't have come to life if it weren't for the contributing farms and schools. Thank you for opening my eyes to "farm to school" and allowing me to work closely with you to change school food. To keep our local food systems sustainable and working on school food reform is what we need to focus on.

The collective energy of everyone else involved created a fantastic momentum that allowed this book to take on a life of its own.

Thank you all!!

Contents

Introduction

Southern California is blessed with a Mediterranean climate in which farmers can grow myriad types of produce year round. Happily, area residents can enjoy the varied bounty every month of the year as we follow the season's produce from farm to table. Southern California's unique topography nurtures a variety of microclimates that support farms all over the region — from coastal Carmel Valley to Imperial Beach, through Jamul, into Escondido, and up to the velvety green countryside of Fallbrook, Valley Center, Rainbow, and even into Temecula. North County boasts the majority of San Diego's farms where gorgeous groves of avocado, citrus, and persimmon trees line the winding roads.

There has long been a charge by San Diego chefs to source locally — to establish relationships with the farmers who grow our food and the people who consume it. A lot of regional chefs are leading the way for the growing national movement that encourages people to eat more locally grown and produced foods. By eating locally, we help sustain our small family farms; we enjoy food that is fresher, more flavorful, and healthier for us; and we help reduce negative effects on the environment. By this simple act of eating well, we benefit our health, our community, and our planet!

This book is partly about telling you the story of family farms and school garden projects that I've had the pleasure of working with. *(See profiles of the schools and farms scattered throughout the book.)* From seed to plant — and from harvest to kitchen — sustainable agriculture and food systems begin with the choices you and I make. The difference between commodity produce and locally grown organic produce comes down to individuals. Locally grown food is all about the farmers and the care with which they approach the product: It's all about the relationship between farmer and soil. Agribusiness, on the other hand, is all about profit — the processes it uses cause a loss of nutrients, flavor, and overall product integrity.

The final chapter of this book discusses many of the most pressing issues we face in making our food choices. It also provides an overview of some of the people and organizations that are working hard to improve school food and nutrition for kids everywhere.

It is my hope that after reading and using this book you'll be excited to shop seasonally, cook simply, and taste the food that is grown near you. If Southern California isn't your home, I hope *From Terra's Table* inspires you to go out and meet the farmers in your hometown and support your local Farmers' Markets. Additionally, get involved with the schools in your area and help shape the way our kids eat at school.

WHERE I COME FROM

No introduction would be complete without a little background about the author, right? Well, here goes: My food journey began when my parents, Mike and Bobbi, moved my sister, Melissa, and me to San Diego in 1975, where my dad pursued a partnership in a specialty wine, cheese, and deli venture. At its peak, the company had 12 stores from San Bernardino to El Cajon in most of the major shopping malls. After my dad and his partners sold off the delicatessens in 1980, they found out about a Mission Valley hotel with a vacant game room and no restaurant. So the following year, my dad filled the game room with a restaurant. (I use that term very loosely, coming from the *deli* business — it was literally a steamer, a deli table, a refrigerator, a freezer, and a microwave for the first few years.) After a while, we added a walk-in cooler and freezer; then, a grill and a hood.

I wish I could tell you some glamorous story about how — from the time I could stand — I was in the kitchen with my grandmothers watching every step, learning traditional family recipes. Unfortunately, that's not how the story goes. I learned from the ground up in a working, professional kitchen. This is where my culinary career began — at the age of 12 — washing dishes in the Pam Pam Café in Mission Valley. I continued working there through high school and, upon graduation, decided to go to the University of California, San Diego. There I joined a fraternity, and during that time knew that I could cook. My good friend Danny and I would go to the Asian markets in Kearny Mesa for sashimi-grade *ahi* (yellowfin tuna), and by the time we were back at our apartment, there were 10 to 15 guys waiting for dinner. Every time I cooked, it was like having

a banquet because a whole bunch of guys would just show up. When I graduated in 1991, I had no idea what to do with an economics degree with an emphasis on math and art history. So, I did the only thing I knew how to do — work in a restaurant. I went back to Pam Pam Café, where I spent the day coming up with specials in the kitchen, and then at night, I would turn around and run the front as manager. Dennis was our lead cook, and he and I would come up with killer specials. We were using *chimichurri* (an Argentinian green sauce generally made with parsley, minced garlic, olive oil, roasted chiles, white or red vinegar, and red pepper flakes) years before it became popular in San Diego restaurants. Eventually, we ended up transforming Pam Pam into a full-service restaurant — adding wraps, skewers, and pastas — and nearly doubling sales that year. At this point, I really began to think about food as a career. I went to Boston for a week and trained under Chef Michael Schlow, who was voted one of *Food & Wine* magazine's Best Chefs in 1996. While I was with him, he really schooled me in the finer details of food and wine. I came back from Boston with an unbelievable appreciation for the culinary arts.

When we opened Terra Restaurant on May 7, 1998, I was actually the general manager running the front of the house. My parents didn't think I had enough experience in the kitchen to be executive chef, so we hired someone who helped us open and then went back to his catering business. The first two years were rocky. We went through a few chefs and were constantly compromising our consistency. I soon realized that we either needed to hire a chef/partner or we needed me to just jump in with both feet, hands, and all the rest. Finally, I told my parents enough was enough; it was time for me to take over the kitchen. I guess it was. I've been there ever since.

THE TERRA WAY

We decided upon the name Terra for the restaurant because *terra* means "earth," and it gave credence to our theme of food from the Americas with influences from South, Central, and North America, as well as Asian influences from Hawaii and California. When we first opened, it was next to impossible to get locally distributed farm-fresh produce (except for buying from Farmers' Markets). Today is a totally different story — we have the ability to buy from more than 20 farms that deliver to my restaurant.

Terra is an unpretentious place, with a very comfortable and quiet atmosphere. Within its walls, I strive every day to make "culinary magic," serving what I sometimes refer to

My mom, Bobbi, enjoying lunch at Terra.

With family (left to right): John Michael at Blue Heron Farm, Aaron at Suzie's Farm, and Jody at Cunningham Organic Farm.

as "good ole American cooking with some contemporary twists" for both Terra, and my catering companies, Shalom Kosher Catering and Terra Catering. In keeping with the philosophy of locally grown food and "California Cuisine," I use only the freshest local ingredients and adapt my menus to the rhythm of the seasons.

Good ingredients are the cornerstone of good cooking. But to be a good cook, you must trust your senses, especially your taste buds, and let the cooking come from within. Using all of your senses is the key to producing a good dish. Watch, listen, smell, touch, and taste. A recipe is simply a list of ingredients with instructions on how to get to the end. Most savory recipes can be altered depending on your individual taste preferences and your inspiration. (Pastry and dessert recipes are different – they are more bound by the laws of chemistry and don't really allow for improvisation.) "Home cooks" are always telling me that they love to "add a little of this and a little of that" while they're creating a dish at home. Well, that's the idea of cooking. You'll come to realize, as I did many years ago, that the pleasure of creation is in the process.

So much of cooking can't be learned by reading recipes from a book. Instead, true culinary skill comes from trying, tasting, and testing – using your own intuition and knowledge. It's a learned process that develops over time. Recipes are like roadmaps, but the real key is technique. Recipes give you the ingredients and the direction, but they don't tell you how to react to the dish. Maybe some of the ingredients you used have a higher salt, fat, or water content than the ones suggested in the recipe. You'll need to rely on your senses as well as your technique and skills to react, and adjust accordingly.

I am the true definition of a self-taught chef. I never went to culinary school – and I've only worked with two chefs in my career. I've truly learned cooking from the ground up – hands on, in a working professional kitchen. Now, after 12 years of teaching cooking classes and feeding locals, celebrities, and visitors, I have decided to share some of my recipes for the first time. To all those people who've eaten at Terra, had me cater a party, or taken one of my cooking classes and begged and pleaded for my recipes, I've always said, "Maybe one of these days I'll spend a year or two and put together a little book for y'all." Well, this is it. I truly hope it gets stained, battered, ripped, and put to great use over and over again for many years to come.

May you have wonderful adventures in the kitchen. Great food makes the world go 'round!

Jeff's Kitchen Advice

THE PANTRY

Maintaining a well-stocked pantry is fundamental to being a well-prepared cook. With interesting ingredients on hand, you're free to be inventive, creative, and to react to your dishes by adding that little something extra when it's needed. Here are some of my most used and favorite items — they're things I'll never be without. Most can be found in grocery stores, but specialty shops or ethnic markets often have more variety.

Salt is perhaps the most important and also controversial flavoring tool in any kitchen toolbox. Whenever I teach a class, we always get into a salt discussion: which to use, if any. A lot of doctors and nutritionists are trying to steer chefs away from using salt for health reasons. I say: "No way." As I tell my students: Salt makes the world go 'round. There's just no substitute.

Here's a short list of salt varieties; each delivers its own distinctive quality to a dish. Kosher salt is the most universal and well known; it's inexpensive and has pure salt flavor. The coarse texture gives it more volume and makes it easy to control when salting food. Sea salts are available as both coarse or fine and are a bit more expensive than kosher salt. They tend to have a marine taste and a milder saltiness. Hawaiian sea salts are either pink, gray, or black and are very rich in trace minerals. Moderately priced, large-flaked Maldon sea salt from England is another great choice for both cooking and finishing. Nowadays, smoked salt is all the rage. There's alderwood, hickory, apple, juniper, elm, and the list goes on. Basically, any smoked salt is considered a finishing salt and can add a degree of complexity and smokiness to any dish. Fleur de sel is harvested in Brittany, France, by hand from the surface of salt beds. Its sweet marine taste and crunchy texture make it a fantastic finishing salt preferred by many top chefs around the world.

Peppercorns, like salt, come in a wide range of flavors and colors and are indispensable as "foundation" seasoning for almost any dish. There are numerous common varieties; each one adds a different dimension to a recipe's flavors. Tellicherry peppercorns are some of the most widely available "gourmet" varieties: There are black, white, red, pink, and green, as well as wood-smoked peppercorns, and peppercorns mixed with other flavorings, such as cayenne or lemon peel.

Good-quality oils are a necessity in any kitchen. In addition to the staple olive oil, you'll probably want to keep some corn, canola, sunflower, and soy or vegetable oil around. I use a variety of oils but prefer to cook with unflavored oils unless I want to impart a little extra flavor in the dish. (I'll often reach for truffle oil or red chili oil to do this.) I usually want the flavor components of a dish to remain as unmasked as possible, so I use "finishing" oils instead. I like avocado, walnut, extra virgin olive, hazelnut, or homemade roasted garlic oils for finishing dishes. Sesame oil is also good to keep on hand for stir-frying or wokking vegetables.

I use a variety of **vinegars**, and there are a lot to choose from. There are fruit-flavored vinegars, Asian rice vinegars, as well as red wine or sherry vinegars. Aged balsamic vinegars from Modena, Italy, are generally sweet, dark colored, and usually sold in small, shapely bottles. Fine aged balsamics are used more as condiments for finishing than as a "salad dressing vinegar." The really high-quality ones are great for drizzling over strawberries, ice cream, or dried or cured meats.

Tomatoes are always nice to keep on hand for those winter months when fresh heirloom tomatoes are unavailable. Sun-dried tomatoes — either dry or in olive oil — add a great touch to pastas, salads, omelets, or even in toppings for bruschetta. Canned San Marzanos from Italy are another fantastic alternative for stews and sauces. If you can't find San Marzanos, try another good-quality imported Italian tomato or even try oven roasting out-of-seaon tomatoes to give them more depth of flavor.

High-quality **dried mushrooms** are always nice to have for emergencies or for nonseasonal cooking.

Canned or dried chiles are always handy, especially if you're into Mexican cooking. Chipotles (smoked jalapeños) in Adobo are widely available canned, but you may also find dried chipotles at Farmers' Markets or specialty stores. Chile de Arbol, Ancho/Pasilla or Guajillo are all excellent to have on hand as well.

A great quality **smoked paprika** is a cousin to Hungarian and is indispensable in any number of shrimp or pork dishes, tapas, and Spanish chorizo. It adds the absolutely perfect taste of authenticity to paellas and is used in American cuisine to season barbecue pork, kebabs, and rich beef and lamb stews. There is no substitute for its use in authentic Spanish cooking.

Garlic pastes such as Sambal (Indonesian chile-garlic paste) or Sriracha (Thai chile-garlic paste) are great to have on hand to give a good, hot, spicy kick to any sauce or dish. Be careful, a little goes a long way. Look for them in your grocery store's Asian section.

Anchovy fillets packed in olive oil add great depth of flavor. Taste them before using; some require rinsing due to saltiness.

Fish sauce is always useful if you're into Asian cooking, especially Thai or Vietnamese.

Low-sodium soy sauce (or Tamari, which is gluten free) is great for salting or marinating.

BASIC COOKING METHODS

Throughout history, humans have always "cooked" their food in one way or another. However, cooking techniques and ingredients have varied by region, reflecting unique environmental, economic, and cultural conditions. The vast majority of cooking, in its simplest form, is the process of preparing food by applying heat. The following are the most common methods for cooking with heat. A general understanding of these techniques, as well as a mastery of them, will greatly enhance your culinary skills and will help to ensure the success of the dishes you prepare.

Baking is a method of fully cooking food by dry heat in an oven. During baking, steam rises from the water content in the ingredients; this steam combines with the dry heat of the oven to cook the food. Different types of ovens do cook differently. A convection oven, for example, circulates hot air constantly during the baking process. This means that convection ovens cook about 25 to 30 percent faster than conventional ovens. To figure out how to compensate for a convection oven over a conventional one, a general rule of thumb would be: Bake for the same length of time as you would using a conventional oven, but reduce the temperature by 25 degrees.

Blanching is a method of quickly cooking raw vegetables in salted, rapidly boiling water for a few moments and then "shocking," or stopping the cooking process, by submerging the vegetables in an ice bath. *(See Chef's Tip, Page 44.)* This process intensifies and preserves the color of most vegetables. After they have been "shocked" in the ice, they must be removed and set on a baking sheet or tray to dry so they don't become waterlogged. It is imperative that before blanching the vegetables be cut into similar-size pieces so they cook evenly.

Braising is a slow-cooking method, usually reserved for tough pieces of meat. A braise is always started first by searing and browning the meat on the stovetop, caramelizing any vegetables, and then adding aromatics along with stock, wine, or other liquid. Searing should be done in the same pot as braising to retain as much flavor and browned bits as possible. All of the ingredients are placed together in a rondeau, or a large, wide-bottomed braising pot, and then slowly cooked until the meat is tender. Tomatoes, wine, beets, apples, cinnamon sticks, and even beer are great ingredients to use for braises. The braising liquid can then be strained, reduced, and used as an excellent sauce. It's much easier to braise items at least one day in advance and then reduce, or boil off, the braising liquid to make the sauce. Cheeks, short ribs, pot roast, brisket, shanks, pork belly, and oxtail all take well to braising. Moroccan tagine and beef bourguignon are great examples of braised dishes.

Frying is believed to have originated in ancient Egypt around 2500 B.C. With this method, oil or other fat is heated to a high temperature and then used to transfer heat to the food. Sautéing, stir-frying, pan frying, wokking, shallow frying, and deep frying are all standard frying techniques that differ in the type of oil, the amount of oil, and the type of pan or vessel used. Different oils can be heated to different temperatures — peanut oil, for example, has a higher smoke point than olive oil — so be aware of the differences in cooking oils and cooking times.

Grilling is a fast method of cooking using radiant heat and is basically the same as broiling. Grilling is done with high, intense heat that caramelizes the food's surface and adds additional flavor complexity. Grilling can be done over heat (e.g., over charcoal or on gas or electric grills) under heat (e.g., under gas or electric grills, under gas or electric salamanders — heat or flame sources that come down from above, usually found in professional kitchens) or between heat (e.g., electrically heated grills, such as a panini press).

Microwaving is a very controversial tool for a chef, but sometimes very useful in the kitchen — though I don't recommend it as a basic cooking technique. Microwaves cook foods from the inside out, which can be handy for certain things (precooking potatoes or vegetables before adding them to a dish) but not ideal for others. In general, a microwave will help you save time with dishes by allowing you to precook, heat, or melt numerous ingredients as you prepare your recipe. A lot of pastry chefs use the microwave to temper chocolate.

Poaching is done in liquid that is just below boiling (when the liquid's surface begins to show some quivering movement). The amount and temperature of the liquid used depends on the food being poached. Meats and poultry are usually simmered in stock; fish is often poached in water, wine, or stock that is flavored with aromatics such as onion, peppercorn, bay leaf, celery, and thyme (this is also known as "court bouillon"); and eggs are commonly poached in lightly salted water, often with a little vinegar added. Fruit is often poached in a light sugar syrup made with water, a little wine, sugar, cinnamon, fruit slices, peppercorns, lemongrass, ginger, and other aromatic flavoring agents. Poaching produces a delicate flavor in foods, while imparting some of the liquid's flavor to the finished product.

Roasting is an oven-cooking method where food is placed in an uncovered pan. Roasting usually produces a well-browned exterior while it preserves a moist interior (it's also a great way to caramelize vegetables). Specialty ovens like a tandoor or a rotisserie can be used for roasting. Roasting requires reasonably tender pieces of meat or poultry. However, roasting a large turkey for the holidays can be done, just on a lower temperature and with occasional basting. Tougher pieces of meat need moist cooking methods such as braising.

Sautéing is a type of frying that cooks food quickly in a pan with fat or oil over direct heat. This method is most commonly

Making my sweet and delicious braised pork belly.

used for foods that have a significant moisture content, such as fresh fruits or vegetables. The term comes from the French word *sauter*, "to jump." When done correctly, the food "jumps" in the pan. When sautéing with butter, it is usually a good idea to add a little oil to prevent the butter from burning. It is imperative to season your food evenly when sautéing, especially when adding liquid or deglazing after the sauté.

Smoking is a great way to add an additional layer of flavor complexity to foods — and you can smoke just about anything. Most smokers work by exposing food to smoke while inside a closed cooker on low heat for a long period of time.

Steaming utilizes the hot gases created by boiling a liquid to gently cook food. This method preserves delicate flavors of food and is perfect for cooking fragile items — such as handmade dumplings — that would fall apart if handled too much by frying or other cooking methods.

Wokking is a specific method of sautéing and stir-frying — done on very high heat — that uses a versatile round-bottomed cooking vessel that originated in China. It is used especially in East and Southeast Asia. Woks are most often used for stir-frying, but they can also be used many other ways, such as in steaming, deep frying, braising, stewing, smoking, or making soup. Wok chefs commonly use a long-handled spatula, or *hoak*, that allows them to stir and mix without burning their hands.

OTHER USEFUL TERMS AND TIPS

Chiffonade. *Chiffon* is French for "rag," which refers to the fabriclike strips that result from this technique. Chiffonade is a technique in which herbs or leafy green vegetables (such as spinach and basil) are cut into long, thin strips. This is generally done by stacking leaves, rolling them tightly, then cutting across the rolled leaves with a sharp knife, producing fine ribbons.

Deglazing. This is a method that uses liquid to remove solids from a pan or pot during cooking. While the surface remains on the heat, a liquid is added (water, wine, broth, stock, etc.) and is used to loosen and dissolve the "sucs," or solid brown pieces stuck to the pan.

Emulsifying means to combine two liquids that normally do not combine easily, such as oil and vinegar. This is done by slowly adding one ingredient to another while whisking rapidly. This disperses and suspends one liquid throughout the other.

Basic Aromatic and Flavoring Combinations: Various aromatic vegetables, seasonings, and flavoring ingredients are often needed to form a "flavor base" in a dish. These elements range from single items to more complex mixtures and are used in many different preparations. One of the most frequently used is *mirepoix*, which is a combination of two parts chopped onion, one part carrot, and one part celery. For a white mirepoix, just substitute leek for the carrot. Traditional southern cooking often calls for the trinity, which is onion, celery, and bell pepper. Depending upon cooking times, the size of the cut will vary. In our stocks, we tend to use a bouquet garni, or sachet — a package of herbs and spices (usually parsley stems, fresh thyme, rosemary, bay leaves, garlic, and black peppercorns) tied in a piece of cheesecloth. This combination of aromatic vegetables, herbs, and spices is meant to provide the background flavors of a dish, not the dominant ones.

Demonstrating how to chiffonade basil.

Basic Plain Pasta Dough Recipe: Ingredients: $1\frac{1}{4}$ cups all-purpose flour, 3 large eggs, 1 ounce olive oil, pinch of salt. First, mound the flour on a work surface or in a large bowl and make a well in the center. Then break the eggs into the well and add the oil and the salt. Using a fork, begin to whisk the eggs and oil together incorporating the flour, little by little. Gradually mix the flour with the eggs, working from the center out. Use your free hand to hold the mound in place and stop any leakage. Knead the dough on a lightly floured surface. The dough should be soft and pliable but dry to the touch. It will take at least 6 minutes kneading to achieve a smooth and elastic texture. Put the dough in a plastic bag without sealing, or cover it with a towel and allow the dough to rest for 30 minutes. You can add basil or any herb to your pasta dough by breaking the eggs into a food processor and adding 3 cups of herbs and processing until smooth. Then pour the eggs into the well and continue with above directions. (*See Heirloom Cherry Tomato Fettucini Recipe, Page 71.*)

Making Pasta: Making pasta isn't difficult, but a few tips will keep you from swearing too much. Make sure your kitchen is well ventilated, without breezes or the air-conditioning blasting. Also, humidity can cause unruly problems, so don't make the dough on a rainy day. Homemade pasta can be stored in the refrigerator for up to 7 days, tightly wrapped in plastic or in an airtight container.

Caramelizing Onions: Cut the onions into $\frac{1}{2}$-inch slices. In a large sauté pan on high heat, add some oil and then the onions. Break up the onions and coat them with the oil. Continue on high heat until the water from the onions has released and evaporated. As soon as the pan is fairly dry, turn down the heat to low. Stir the onions so all pieces get equal time making direct contact with the pan: if onion pieces are on top of each other they will not brown. Some people cheat by adding sugar, but there's plenty of sugar in the onions to give you a really nice caramelized color and flavor.

Simple Syrup Recipe: Bring equal parts sugar and water to a boil to dissolve the sugar. Turn off heat, then add flavoring agents, if desired, while syrup is still hot but not boiling. Try enhancing with fruit, ginger, lemongrass, cinnamon, star anise, mint, or even basil or rosemary.

Stocks & Remouillage: Brown stocks are made from roasted bones, generally veal bones (sometimes chicken bones), roasted vegetables, and tomato paste. White stocks are made from uncooked bones (even from fish), white mirepoix, and no tomato paste. A *remouillage*, meaning "rewetting" or second wash of the bones, is made by taking the bones from the primary stock after being strained, then adding fresh water, herbs, and vegetables, and starting the stock again.

The remouillage has less flavor than a stock, but it has flavor nonetheless — which is better than plain water. Vegetable stocks are made using the same methods for brown and white stocks (but without the bones!).

Making Stocks the Classical Way: Maintaining the proper ratio of bones to water is crucial for making an excellent-quality stock. For beef, veal, poultry, or game stocks, here's the basic rule of thumb: To make 1 gallon of stock, use 8 pounds of bones, 6 quarts of water, 1 pound mirepoix and 1 standard bouquet garni. It is important to combine the bones with cool water and bring the water slowly to a boil, but then to reduce the heat to a simmer if the stock continues to boil. Any blood or impurities will cloud the stock. Constant skimming of the impurities will determine how clear the final stock is. After 1 hour, add the flavoring ingredients. Spices and herbs will generally release their flavor sufficiently after about 15 to 30 minutes. Other flavoring ingredients can be added to simmer as well (ginger, mushrooms, tomatoes, wines, etc.). Brown stocks generally take about 6 to 8 hours of simmering time. White and brown poultry stocks should be allowed a minimum of 3 hours, and vegetable or seafood stocks (*See Chef's Tip: Cooking Lobster, Page 86*) need about 1 hour. Many chefs will take a finished stock and use it as a flavorful poaching liquid or as a base in soups and stews. Beef and chicken stocks can be reduced by a little over a half — to a "demi-glace" — at which point they are thicker and have a more concentrated flavor. Demi-glaces are often used as a base for sauces. If a demi-glace is reduced again — roughly by half — it will thicken to a gelatinous consistency when cool. This is called a "glace" and can also be used as the foundation of a sauce or in other recipes where an intense, rich flavor is called for.

Soups: As far as I'm concerned, the seasons dictate which soups to make when. Spring soups can capitalize on fresh vegetables like asparagus, green peas, and seasonal mushrooms. Summer soups can be cool and refreshing, like gazpachos or cold fruit and cold vegetable soups. Fall and winter soups — like chili, chowders, and stews — utilize legumes and root vegetables and are usually much heartier — perfect for colder weather! Whether you're making soups, bisques, chowders, consommés, or cold soups, the basic skills are the same. All these dishes require the right balance of liquid to solid ingredients, as well as the right level of thickness and flavor intensity. Often, the ingredients that go into these recipes vary significantly in volume, water content, and flavor concentration. In many cases, you will need to get your soup completely assembled, let it cook for a little while, then taste, season, and thicken as needed. Remember, trust your senses, and always use your great stocks as a base.

Making latkes with my dad, Mike.

MEASUREMENT EQUIVALENTS

It's always helpful to have a handy reference of measurements close by.

1 tablespoon = 3 teaspoons	3/8 cup = 6 tablespoons	8 fluid ounces = 1 cup
1/16 cup = 1 tablespoon	1/2 cup = 8 tablespoons	1 pint = 2 cups
1/8 cup = 2 tablespoons	2/3 cup = 10 tablespoons + 2 teaspoons	1 quart = 2 pints
1/6 cup = 2 tablespoons + 2 teaspoons	3/4 cup = 12 tablespoons	1 quart = 4 cups
1/4 cup = 4 tablespoons	1 cup = 48 teaspoons	1 gallon = 4 quarts
1/3 cup = 5 tablespoons + 1 teaspoon	1 cup = 16 tablespoons	16 dry ounces = 1 pound

I'll admit it: This recipe is included here purely as a way to pander to popular demand. We didn't really have a natural place for it in the following chapters, but I know that there are scads of people who would be very upset with me if I left this one out. It's a major customer favorite. (Thanks to former Terra chef Neil Stuart, who originally created this recipe.) So here it is. It takes a little patience, but the finished product is well worth it.

TERRA'S FAMOUS CHOCOLATE CIGAR

Yields 26 • Total time: Overnight / Active: 90 minutes

1½	quarts	heavy whipping cream
2	pounds	bittersweet or semisweet chocolate
¾	pound	butter
1	tablespoon	vanilla
1	package	phyllo dough*
½	cup	canola oil
		cocoa powder (for dusting)

1. In a medium stock pot, bring 1 quart of cream to a boil. Remove from heat, add chocolate and ¼ pound of the butter, and stir until completely melted and combined. Stir in vanilla. Line an 8-inch x 11-inch baking dish with plastic wrap, pour the chocolate mix into the dish, and place in the refrigerator until semifirm. (IMPORTANT: Make sure the pan is level.) Put into the freezer overnight.

2. On a clean cutting board, turn chocolate out and remove plastic wrap. The size of your cigars will depend on your cuts, so make your cuts accordingly. Cut the slab of chocolate in half lengthwise and then make crosswise cuts about 1 inch apart. You should wind up with about 26 pieces.

3. For the wrapping process you will need a clean, damp towel, a pastry brush, and a wax paper-lined baking sheet sprayed with nonstick spray. In a small sauce pot on medium-low heat, melt the remaining ½ pound of butter. On another clean cutting board, lay out the phyllo dough and place the damp towel over it to keep the dough moist. (Phyllo dough can dry out very quickly and lose its flexibility.) Take 2 sheets of dough, brush them liberally with butter, and place a chocolate log onto the dough about 1 inch from the bottom end of the sheet. Begin wrapping the chocolate by lifting the bottom over the chocolate and then rolling the covered chocolate one time. Brush with a little more butter and fold in the ends. Roll again and then fold in the ends. Brush with butter and repeat the process until the chocolate is fully wrapped. Brush the whole "cigar" with more butter and set it on top of the baking sheet. Repeat this process with the remaining cigars. Cover with plastic wrap and return them to the freezer until ready to cook. (At this point, they can be stored in the freezer up to 1 month.)

4. Heat a sauté pan with canola oil on medium-high heat. With a pair of kitchen tongs, place 1, 2, or 3 cigars in the oil and sauté on each side until brown. Lower the heat to low and continue to sauté the cigars while rotating them, so the phyllo doesn't burn. When cigar feels tender inside, the chocolate is hot enough and will melt when cut.

5. Whip the remaining ½ quart of cream and serve each cigar on a cloud of the whipped cream and dust with cocoa powder. No need for sweetened whipped cream because the chocolate is so rich.

Throughout this book, you will find some ingredients marked with an asterisk (*).
For more information on where to purchase these ingredients, see our Product Resource Guide, page 204.

Wine Advice

For some reason, wine intimidates a lot of people. Beer doesn't. Vodka doesn't. Tequila doesn't. But when it comes to ordering, buying, pairing, or discussing wine, people get nervous. So, the first thing to remember is that wine is really no different from any other beverage — if you like it, it's good. As far as pairing goes, wine experts have put a lot of "rules" out there, but the same caveat applies to pairing food and wine: if you like it, it's a good pairing. Everyone's palate is different, and what may taste like a fabulous match to a sommelier at a 5-star restaurant may taste lousy to you.

With all of the above having been said, this book offers suggestions to guide you if you're interested in pairing the recipes with either wine or beer. The suggestions are just that: They are by no means intended to be the only possible pairings, and they may not mesh with your palate. They're simply meant to be a starting point. Each suggestion is made in 2 parts: suggested styles of wine (a grape variety or type) followed by a few specific labels. The specific wines are by no means the only wines that will work — they are meant to highlight local and California wineries and to give you specific guidance, if that's what you want or need. If you don't like a pairing — then explore others on your own.

As a quick reference, the lists below offer descriptives of the most widely available California varietals of whites and reds. They are listed in order of "heaviness" or "richness" — the top of each list being the lightest and gaining in weight, body, and (often) alcohol as you move down.

WHITES

- **Pinot Gris:** light, high acidity
- **Chenin Blanc:** light, high acidity (some are sweet)
- **Riesling and Gewürztraminer:** light-medium, high acidity ("late harvest" varieties are sweet)
- **Sauvignon Blanc:** varies widely in style from "light and grassy" to "oaky"
- **Viognier, Marsanne, Roussanne:** Medium-bodied with medium acidity
- **Chardonnay:** varies widely in style, from medium-bodied to heavier and oaky with medium to low acidity

REDS

- **Rosé:** light, high acidity (some vinified sweet)
- **Pinot Noir:** medium, high acidity
- **Sangiovese:** medium, medium acidity
- **Tempranillo:** medium, medium acidity
- **Grenache, Mourvèdre, Malbec, Cabernet Franc:** medium to semi-heavy, medium acidity
- **Merlot:** ranges from medium to rich, full-bodied with lower relative acidity
- **Cabernet Sauvignon:** ranges from medium to rich and full-bodied, lower relative acidity
- **Zinfandel:** ranges from light-medium to heavy-bodied ("old vine"), low relative acidity
- **Syrah:** commonly rich and full-bodied with low relative acidity

Beer Advice

To simplify the sheer magnitude of available beer styles, consider categorizing them into the 2 major groups: ales and lagers. There are many distinguishing differences between these 2 major beer categories, but the essential difference lies in yeast and fermentation. In a nutshell, ale yeast ferments at a higher temperature and produces fruity and spicy flavors, while lager yeast ferments at a cooler temperature and yields crisper, cleaner-finishing beers.

GENERAL FOOD-PAIRING GUIDELINES

There are many different approaches to planning successful beer and food pairings, but the general rules are rather simple. Identify what you want to accomplish first, and build on that idea when searching for the right beer. Beer can complement the flavors of a dish by bridging similar flavors together, can contrast with foods by combining different flavors, or can simply be used as a palate cleanser.

TYPES OF LAGER

- **Crisp & Dry (Pilsner, Helles, Dortmunder):** These crisp, golden lagers will vary in hops character but will be consistent in body and toasted malt flavors. They're great additions to richer fare, as their dry effervescence will refresh the palate.
- **Smooth & Malty (Oktoberfest/Marzen, Maibock, Amber Lager):** These malt-forward lagers provide a wealth of caramel, toasted, and nutty malt flavors to pair with. They're ideal to match with the caramelized flavors of grilled meats or the toasted flavors of fresh breads and pizzas.
- **Dark & Roasted (Schwarzbier & Black Lager):** Generous additions of dark malts give these medium-bodied beers roasted, chocolate, and coffee malt flavors. They're great additions to BBQ and can even hold their own at the dessert table.
- **Full-bodied & Robust (Bockbier):** These strong lagers range in alcohol from 6 to 10 percent and have rich caramel and toasted malt flavors. Hop bitterness takes a backseat to forward-malt flavors that pair especially well with roasted meats and tangier cheeses.

TYPES OF ALE

- **Malty & Mild (Amber, Brown & Red Ale, ESB, Scottish Ale, Altbier):** These malt-centric styles provide an ample amount of caramel and toasted flavors to pair with. Hops character tends to be mild and won't overpower delicately spiced foods.
- **Fruity & Spicy (Saison, Tripel, Witbier, Bavarian Hefeweizen):** Warm fermentations give these beers prominent fruity flavors and varying degrees of spice. These beers make excellent complements to dishes that incorporate fresh fruit, and their effervescence makes them great palate cleansers.
- **Fruity & Hoppy (American Pale, Belgian Pale, English IPA):** The balance of malt and hops makes these styles versatile when pairing with food. They're hoppy enough to temper spice, and possess an array of fruity and malty characteristics to complement many foods.
- **Very Hoppy (American IPA, American IIPA, Black IPA):** The intense hop bitterness of these styles makes them ideal for tempering assertively spiced dishes. The citrus character of American hops makes them excellent additions to Mexican and Thai-inspired dishes.
- **Dark & Roasted (Stout & Porter):** These beers are traditionally brewed with darker malts that lend rich chocolate, roasted, and coffee flavors to the beer. Depending on the brand, hops character and fruitiness can range from mild to prominent. They're great with roasted meats and chocolate desserts.
- **Full-bodied & Robust (Barleywine, Wee Heavy, Belgian Strong):** These rich ales possess varying degrees of hops bitterness but are consistent in their strong fruity and malty character. They're terrific aperitifs or after-dinner additions.

avocados

IN THE MONTHS FROM MAY TO AUGUST, California produces 90 percent of the nation's avocados. Roughly 60 percent of those come from San Diego County, the undisputed avocado capital of the United States. California avocados are hand grown on more than 6,000 small family farms throughout Central and Southern California. These growers, and their passion and dedication to sustainable agriculture, truly make California avocados a premium fruit. There are 8 varieties of commercially grown avocados in California, but the Hass represents 95 percent of the total crop volume. The other varieties are the Bacon, Fuerte, Gwen, Lamb Hass, Pinkerton, Reed, and Zutano.

Here are a few helpful hints for working with this silky and luscious fruit.

• When selecting avocados, the first thing to remember is that the prettiest skin color doesn't necessarily mean the best fruit. Hass avocados turn almost black as they ripen, while other varieties remain a bright green. Once you've spotted a possible candidate, gently squeeze the fruit in the palm of your hand. The fruit should be firm, but should yield a little softness. If you get some avocados that need ripening assistance, place them in a brown paper bag with an orange, apple, or a banana for a couple of days. Make sure to check the bag each day, so the avocados don't get overripe.

• Before cutting an avocado, first wash the outside thoroughly and place it on a clean work surface. Then make a horizontal slice to the seed, rotate the avocado around the blade of the knife, and then twist the avocado to separate the halves. Remove the seed by sliding the tip of a spoon gently underneath and lifting it out. Scoop out the pulp and either slice, dice, mash, or reserve. Make sure to sprinkle some lime or lemon juice on the outside surface of the pulp so it doesn't oxidize and turn black. If you're mashing the avocado into guacamole, cover the entire top of the guacamole directly with plastic wrap, pushing out all of the air. Avocados are amazingly versatile and can be easily frozen — they're great for salsas, soups, sandwiches, or in sorbet.

GUACAMOLE DE PIMIENTO

Yields 1 quart • Total time: 1 hour / Active: 1 hour

Early in 2009, I got an assignment from the California Avocado Commission. They wanted me to come up with a new version of the Southern California guacamole that I had previously developed for them. I love roasted peppers and chiles, and I really wanted a way to combine the roasted flavors with the creaminess of the avocado. That's how I came up with this recipe. Because of the roasted nature of the chiles, this guacamole will not be bright green, but it will have intense flavor.

2		poblano chiles, roasted *(See Chef's Tip, Below)*
1		jalapeño, roasted *(See Chef's Tip, Below)*
1		red bell pepper, roasted *(See Chef's Tip, Below)*
1		medium red onion
4		medium Hass avocados
2	tablespoons	fresh lime juice
1	teaspoon	ground cumin
½	cup	fresh cilantro, chopped
		salt and pepper to taste

1. Dice the roasted chiles and peppers very small. Reserve. Chop the onion and caramelize on low heat in a medium sauté pan. In a bowl, mash the avocado and combine it with the chiles, onions, and remaining ingredients. Season with salt and pepper.

Chef's Tip: Roasting Chiles and Peppers: You can roast chiles and peppers under the broiler, on a very hot grill, over an open fire, or on a gas stove top with an open flame. Before roasting, clean the chiles and dry them thoroughly. Get the heat source ready. Place the chiles under or over the heat and turn them every minute or so until the skin is blackened. The entire chile should be black and charred. This should take about 5 minutes. Carefully remove the chiles from the heat, place them in a plastic bag, and seal it. Let the chiles "sweat" like this for 10 to 15 minutes. This will make the skins easier to remove. (You can also place the chiles in a plastic storage container with a lid, or on a plate covered with plastic wrap or a towel.) One at a time, rub the outside of the chiles to remove the skins. (Some people remove the skins while holding the chile under running water. The water can remove some of the flavorful oils in the chile so try to remove the skins with just your fingers.) Use a knife to remove any skin that sticks. Remove the seeds, too. When the chiles are all peeled, you can refrigerate them for later or use them immediately for the best flavor.

To Drink with Your Meal...

Wine: The spice of the chiles and the piquancy of the onions make this dish a perfect match for a crisp, minerally, fruit-forward wine, such as a **Riesling, Fumé,** or **Sauvignon Blanc**.
- Orfila White Riesling
- Ferrari-Carano Fumé

Beer: While many beer styles will pair with guacamole, few refresh the palate better than a crisp Czech-style or German **Pilsner**.
- Karl Strauss Woodie Gold
- Victory Prima Pils

To Drink with Your Meal…

Wine: The flavors of mango, lime, and cilantro will pair well with a medium-bodied white, such as a **Chardonnay** or a **Viognier.**
- Milagro Farm Chardonnay
- Rosenblum "Kathy's Cuvée" Viognier

Beer: The sweet caramel malt character of an **Amber Lager/Ale** will complement the grilled chicken without overpowering the more delicate flavors.
- Brooklyn Lager
- Ballast Point Calico Amber

ACHIOTE CHICKEN TOSTADA WITH AVOCADO–GOAT CHEESE MOUSSE

Serves 4 to 6 • Total time: 6 to 24 hours / Active: 1 hour

Annatto is a seed that is used as a spice and coloring agent (for desserts, butter, and cheeses and a natural dye for cosmetics and textiles) and to make achiote paste in Latin cuisines. The Maya Indians of Central America used the bright dye as war paint. On Mexico's Yucatán Peninsula, annatto seeds* are ground together with chiles, garlic, bitter orange, and other spices to make a rub called achiote paste for whole suckling pig. The "cochinita pibil," or pig, is then wrapped in banana leaves and slowly cooked in a stone-lined pit. Annatto seed, like turmeric, is best known for its color. It can enrich the look of sauces and stews beyond the rust color of its seeds — its delicious golden oil can enliven your cooking!

ACHIOTE MARINADE

½	cup	achiote paste*
1	cup	fresh orange juice
½	tablespoon	fresh garlic, minced
½	tablespoon	fresh oregano, chopped
¼	cup	olive oil
¼	cup	fresh cilantro, chopped
		salt and pepper to taste
2	4- to 6-ounce	boneless, skinless chicken breasts

AVOCADO–GOAT CHEESE MOUSSE

5 to 6		medium Hass avocados, diced roughly
½	cup	goat cheese
1¾	cup	heavy whipping cream
2	teaspoons	kosher salt
¼	teaspoon	cayenne pepper
2	teaspoons	fresh lemon juice

MANGO-LIME SLAW

3	cups	mango purée *(See Recipe, Page 146)*
¾	cup	fresh lime juice
1	bunch	fresh cilantro
¼	cup	honey
¼	cup	sour cream
1	teaspoon	kosher salt
1	head	Napa cabbage

TOSTADA

15		round gyoza/potsticker wrappers*
		cilantro, chopped (for garnish)

1. Make the marinade. Combine the first 2 ingredients in a bowl. With a whisk, break up the paste. Add the remaining ingredients and season with salt and pepper. Marinate the chicken for 6 to 24 hours.

CONTINUED >

2. Make the avocado–goat cheese mousse. Place avocado, goat cheese, ¼ cup cream, salt, cayenne, and lemon juice into a food processor. Purée until smooth. Put the remaining 1½ cups cream into a bowl. Whip with a whisk until soft peaks are formed. Fold into the avocado mixture and reserve for service, refrigerated.

3. Preheat oven to 375°F.

4. Lightly spray or brush canola oil onto the wrappers and bake for about 10 minutes, or until golden brown. Alternatively, fry wrappers in oil in a sauce pot or fryer.

5. Make the mango-lime slaw. Place all ingredients, except cabbage, in a blender and purée for about 30 seconds. Cut the cabbage into slawlike strips, toss with vinaigrette, and place on each "tostada."

6. Grill the chicken and place a slice or two on top of the cabbage. Top with the mousse, garnish with cilantro, and serve.

Stehly Farms Organics

The coolest thing you notice when you visit Stehly Farms is that they're a big operation that still manages to feel small. The two Stehly brothers that own and operate the business – Noel and Jerome – call their farm a "small family-owned company," but they harvest organic produce across thousands of acres in northern San Diego County. One 300-acre ranch in Valley Center has been farmed by the Stehlys since the family bought the land more than 45 years ago.

The Stehlys focus on growing, packing, and distributing certified organic avocados, citrus, and berries. They grow four varieties of avocados (Bacon, Hass, Fuerte, and Reed); four varieties of berries (blackberries, golden raspberries, blueberries, and red raspberries); two varieties of grapefruit (Star Ruby and Marsh Ruby); two varieties of lemons (Meyer and Eureka); two varieties of limes (Bearss and Sweet); two varieties of oranges (Navel and Valencia); and incredibly delicious Manzano chiles. All told, Stehly Farms grows millions of pounds of amazing fruit every year.

As you may imagine, Noel and Jerome are somewhat tickled that demand for organic produce has skyrocketed in recent years. Thanks in part to the Slow Food Movement, people all across America have become more aware of the value of organic foods that are locally grown. The boom in organics has enabled Stehly to expand outside California and to get into many national markets. In addition to Farmers' Markets all across San Diego, Orange, and Los Angeles counties, Stehly produce can be found at Whole Foods, Jimbo's Naturally, Barons Marketplace, and many other quality food locations.

More information about Stehly Farms Organics is included in Featured Organic Farms on page 202.

Above: Tomatoes in a hothouse. Below (left to right): Zoe the Australian shepherd, Noel, and Jerome give me a tour of their beautiful Valley Center farm; rich, flavorful avocado oil made next door by Bella Vado from Stehly fruit; just-picked Hass avocados rumble through the sorter before packing.

LEMON AVOCADO OIL–MARINATED FLANK STEAK WITH AVOCADO CHIMICHURRI

Serves 8 • Total time: 12 to 24 hours / Active: 45 minutes

I first used chimichurri — an Argentinian parsley garlic sauce — at my other restaurant, Pam Pam. That was way back in 1995, before chimichurri became all the rage. This sauce has a tart characteristic from the vinegar, but the creaminess of the avocado makes it a velvety treat. Also give it a try on chicken or as a dip.

AVOCADO CHIMICHURRI

1	bunch	fresh cilantro
1	bunch	fresh Italian parsley
1½	cups	rice vinegar
1	tablespoon	fresh garlic, chopped
2	teaspoons	fresh oregano
¼	cup	fresh lime juice
2		poblano peppers, roasted *(See Chef's Tip, Page 27)*
2		medium Hass avocados, diced
1	teaspoon	red chile flakes
¾	cup	water
1	teaspoon	kosher salt
½	cup	olive oil

LEMON AVOCADO OIL MARINADE

1½	cups	lemon avocado oil*
½	cup	fresh lemon juice
4	tablespoons	fresh cilantro, chopped
4	pounds	flank steak (or any other steak of your choice)
		salt and pepper to taste

1. In a food processor, combine all the avocado chimichurri ingredients except the oil. While the food processor is on, add the oil in a slow, steady stream. This can be made 1 or 2 days in advance.

2. Make the lemon avocado oil marinade. In a large bowl, combine oil, lemon juice, and cilantro. Add the flank steak and marinate 12 to 24 hours. (Marinating time will depend upon the thickness of the steak you use if other than flank or skirt.)

3. Grill the steaks to the desired doneness, and serve with the avocado chimichurri.

Chef's Tip: Marinades: Marinades add flavor, moisture, and also tenderize meats, poultry, and seafood. Marinades typically include an oil and an acid, but the sky's the limit for creativity. I use orange juice and fresh herbs a lot, but add your own twist with spices, chile peppers, onions, shallots, garlic, ginger, citrus zest, prepared condiments like mustard, ketchup, or plum sauce. For your oil base, try olive, peanut, sesame, walnut, or chile oil. You can also use milk, coconut milk, buttermilk, or yogurt. However, don't add salt to the marinades because it will leach out moisture, drying and toughening what you're preparing. The amount of acid used in your marinade really depends on what you're marinating and how long you have before you cook. If you marinate too long, delicate items like seafood and skinless chicken can actually begin to cook and become mushy from the acid. Remember, always marinate in the refrigerator to avoid the growth of bacteria, and discard the marinade after it has been used. However, if you intend to use the same mixture to baste, either set aside a small amount before marinating or boil the marinade for 5 minutes before using it as a basting sauce.

To Drink with Your Meal...

Wine: Grilled or broiled steak is always a good match with a medium to full-bodied red. With this sauce, a **Cabernet Franc** or **Merlot** would pair beautifully.
• Titus Cabernet Franc
• Fallbrook 33° North Merlot

Beer: Grilled meats are a natural fit with malt-centric beers, but the citrus elements in this dish will be enhanced by a **Pale Ale** with good hops character.
• Firestone Walker DBA
• New Belgium Mighty Arrow

All About Avocados

Information from the California Avocado Commission

The California Avocado Commission has a great website (www.CaliforniaAvocado.com) where you can find more facts about avocados, get recipes, read profiles of growers, and get information about the California Avocado industry. You also can follow them on Facebook (www.facebook.com/CaliforniaAvocados) or on Twitter (www.twitter.com/CA_Avocados).

In the United States, the avocado has seen a steady rise in popularity during the past decade. From about 2002 to 2010, overall U.S. per-capita consumption of avocados has doubled. While U.S. consumption peaks during football's "Big Game" day every January and Cinco de Mayo festivities in the form of guacamole, Americans have become fond of eating avocados in many other ways — particularly in salads and on sandwiches. About 50 percent of all U.S. households consume avocados — 80 percent of households on the West Coast.

California is the nation's largest producer of avocados (it supplies about 90 percent of the U.S. market) and is the world's second-largest producer. (Mexico is the largest.)

Today, about 90 percent of California Avocados are the Hass variety. These avocados and 7 other varieties are hand-grown on approximately 60,000 acres throughout Central and Southern California by nearly 6,000 avocado growers, mostly on small family farms. California Avocado growers take advantage of the coastal climate and ideal growing conditions of the region.

EVERY HASS AVOCADO IN THE WORLD CAN TRACE ITS ROOTS TO CALIFORNIA

California postal worker Rudolph Hass first planted avocado seeds at his home in La Habra Heights in 1926. After a couple of unsuccessful attempts to graft the plants with a Fuerte avocado tree, Hass left them alone. When he finally tasted the fruit from the tree he grew, it was creamy, hearty, and delicious. In fact, it was so special that he patented the variety in 1935, naming it Hass, after himself. Word of the Hass avocado's delicious flavor spread throughout California and abroad, and today it is the most popular avocado in the world. The original tree that Hass planted — commonly referred to as "the Mother Hass Tree" is no longer with us. Today, the Hass variety accounts for about 80 percent of all avocados eaten worldwide — each one a descendant of the original California Mother Hass Tree. So even though her fruit has spread around the world, her roots will always be in California.

AMAZING AVOCADO FACTS

Here are some fun and interesting facts that will make you an instant avocado expert:

- Avocados are fruits, not vegetables.
- There are about 500 varieties of avocado, but the vast majority of all avocados grown in the world are the Hass variety.
- Avocados are also called alligator pears, because of their green, bumpy skin.
- A single California Avocado tree can produce up to 500 avocados in a year (200 pounds of fruit).
- On average, Americans consume about 50 million pounds of guacamole during football's "Big Game" day every January — that's enough to cover a football field more than 20-feet deep.
- In Brazil, they add avocados to ice cream.
- In the Philippines, a popular sweet dessert drink is made with avocado, sugar, and condensed milk.
- The average avocado contains 250 calories and 25 grams of healthy polyunsaturated and monounsaturated fat.
- Avocados are naturally cholesterol- and sodium-free.
- Avocados naturally contain many of the vitamins the body needs: vitamins A, C, D, E, K, and the B vitamins (thiamine, riboflavin, niacin, pantothenic acid, biotin, vitamin B-6, vitamin B-12, and folate).
- Avocados contribute good fats to your diet, providing 3 grams of mono and 0.5 gram polyunsaturated fat per 1 ounce serving.

AVOCADO DAIQUIRI

Serves 4 • Total time: 40 minutes / Active: 20 minutes

I created this drink for the California Avocado Commission. Feel free to swap out the rum with tequila for an avocado margarita, or omit the alcohol altogether and serve this treat to the kids.

LEMONGRASS SIMPLE SYRUP

1	cup	granulated sugar
1	cup	water
½	cup	lemongrass, mashed, and chopped

DAIQUIRI

1		medium California Hass Avocado, diced
3	ounces	fresh lime juice
4	cups	crushed ice
6	ounces	light rum
2	ounces	lemongrass simple syrup
4		lime or avocado wedges (for garnish)

1. Make simple syrup. In a medium sauce pan, bring the sugar and water to a boil. Add lemongrass and let simmer for about 3 minutes. Let the syrup sit for about 20 minutes and then pour through a fine mesh strainer to remove any solids. Cool syrup completely. Syrup may be made up to 1 week ahead, kept chilled and covered.

2. Make daiquiri. In a blender, purée avocado, juice, ice, rum, and simple syrup until smooth. Pour into a glass and garnish with a lime or avocado wedge.

CHIPOTLE STEAK SLIDERS WITH AVOCADO-FENNEL AIOLI

Serves 6 (as an appetizer) • Total time: 24+ hours / Active: 2 hours

The California Avocado Commission has asked me numerous times to help them with chef demos at the annual Produce Marketing Convention. This recipe was developed to showcase the many ways California avocados can be prepared. The avocado chimichurri (See Recipe, Page 33) can be substituted for the aioli, and, if you feel like caramelizing some shallots or onions, they add an awesome touch.

CHIPOTLE MARINADE

3		chipotle chiles with adobo sauce *
1	bunch	fresh cilantro
1	6-ounce can	tomato paste
¼	cup	fresh lime juice
2	cups	fresh orange juice
½	cup	brown sugar
2	tablespoons	honey
½	teaspoon	kosher salt
10	cloves	fresh garlic

AVOCADO-FENNEL AIOLI

1	bulb	fennel
3		medium Hass avocados, diced
½	cup	sour cream
½	cup	mayonnaise
¼	cup	fresh basil, chopped
¼	cup	fresh cilantro, chopped
2	tablespoons	fresh lime juice
1		jalapeño, seeded and minced
2	tablespoons	fennel seed
		salt and pepper to taste

TEMPURA BATTER FOR AVOCADO SLICES

½	cup	flour
½	cup	cornstarch
1	teaspoon	baking soda
1	teaspoon	baking powder
1	teaspoon	granulated sugar
½	teaspoon	salt
1		egg
⅔	cup	ice water
		yellow food coloring (optional)

STEAK

1	pound	skirt steak, flank steak, or flat iron steak
		canola or vegetable oil (for deep frying avocado)
1		medium Hass avocado, peeled and cut into 6 wedges to be fried
12		slider buns *
		pea sprouts or microgreens (for garnish)

CONTINUED >

To Drink with Your Meal…

Wine: The smokiness and spiciness of the grilling and the chiles will match well with a heavy-bodied wine such as a **Syrah** or a lighter-style **Sangiovese**.
- Fallbrook 33° North Syrah
- Shafer Sangiovese

Beer: To draw out and enhance the smokiness, try a **Rauchbier** or **Smoked Porter**.
- Alaskan Smoked Porter
- Ballast Point Abandon Ship

1. Purée all the marinade ingredients in a blender. The marinade can keep for 1 to 2 weeks in the refrigerator or frozen for up to 3 months. Marinate the steak for 12 to 24 hours.

2. Make the aioli the day before to let flavors come together for at least 24 hours. Slice the fennel bulb and caramelize it on low heat in a medium sauté pan. In a bowl, mash the avocados with a fork. Combine all ingredients in a food processor and purée until smooth; season with salt and pepper.

3. Make the tempura batter. Sift together the dry ingredients and set aside. In a medium bowl, beat the egg slightly and mix with the ice water. Stir in the dry ingredients. Stir only until just mixed; the mixture will be slightly lumpy.

4. While you are preparing your grill and grilling your steak, tempura fry the avocado. Dip avocado wedges into the batter and deep fry until golden brown. Drain on paper towels.

5. Once your steak is grilled to the desired doneness, let it rest for 5 minutes before slicing.

6. To plate: Spread aioli on slider buns, top with the sliced steak, avocado tempura, a little more aioli, and garnish with pea sprouts.

Chatting with cofounder of Levana's Garden, Nan Sterman, as students Joel Harris, my son Aaron, and Benjamin Harris help out.

San Diego Jewish Academy

At San Diego Jewish Academy, the gorgeous 5,000-square-foot garden is about much more than learning about plants, insects, conservation, nutrition, biology, composting, weather, and life cycles. Levana's Garden (*Gan Levana* in Hebrew) also offers students a chance to enrich their understanding of Judaism and even to use the space to help in the practice and observance of their faith.

Part of the garden is dedicated to growing the six "species" of Israel, each mentioned in the Bible: grapes, dates, figs, olives, almonds, and pomegranates. Another section is an open-air amphitheater used for classes in art and poetry as well as for prayer.

Of course, the garden provides students with great firsthand knowledge and experience in growing their own healthy, organic food. In seven raised beds, younger students grow vegetables, fruits, and herbs for eating on the spot or for use in the school kitchen. Two other areas include a grove of citrus (lemon, lime, orange, and a Jewish ceremonial citron known as *etrog*) and a grove of stone fruits (apples, plums, and nectarines).

Teaching science is also a big part of the garden's objective. The greenhouse is dedicated to growing seedlings and doing experiments. Another area houses a butterfly garden that supports one of the students' science lessons.

The garden is dedicated to the memory of Levana Estline, who was a beloved kindergarten teacher at the academy. Mrs. Estline passed away in 2003, while the students were planning the garden. Those who remember Mrs. Estline fondly recall how her positive attitude and beautiful smile endeared her to students and colleagues alike. She was well known for inspirational sayings, many of which are etched into large boulders throughout the garden.

AVOCADO, CRAB, AND CORN FRITTERS WITH AVOCADO-MANGO SAUCE

Yields 14 (2½-ounce) fritters • Total time: 70 minutes / Active: 70 minutes

Every January just before the Super Bowl I used to hold cooking classes to showcase the many different ways to use avocados. When the California Avocado Commission found out about my classes, they asked me to do some recipe development, and I created this recipe for them for the 2003 Super Bowl media event held in San Diego.

AVOCADO-MANGO SAUCE

½	cup	mango purée *(See Recipe, Page 146)*
½		medium Hass avocado
1	teaspoon	rice wine vinegar

FRITTERS

1		shallot, peeled and finely minced
8	tablespoons	unsalted butter, melted
2		large eggs
1	tablespoon	all-purpose flour
1	tablespoon	baking powder
1	pound	lump crab
3		scallions, thinly sliced
1	cup	fresh corn, cut off the cob
1½		medium Hass avocados, ½-inch dice
1		lemon, zest
1	tablespoon	fresh dill, chopped
1	cup	Panko bread crumbs
4	cups	canola or vegetable oil (for frying)
1		shallot, sliced into rings (for garnish)
		flour (for dusting shallot garnish)
		parsley, chopped (for garnish)

1. To make the avocado-mango sauce, combine the mango purée, avocado, and rice wine vinegar in a blender and purée until smooth. Reserve for service.

2. In a small sauté pan, sauté the shallot in 1 tablespoon of butter until translucent. Remove from heat.

3. In a medium bowl, gently beat the eggs. Add the shallot, remaining butter and ingredients and gently stir together. Don't overmix or the crab will break up. Form the mixture into small balls and reserve on a baking sheet or platter. In a medium sauce pot, heat the oil to 375°F. Gently drop a few of the crab-avocado balls at a time into the oil and fry until golden brown.

4. Lightly dust shallot rings in flour, drop the rings into the hot oil and cook until light brown and crisp.

5. To plate: Place 2 or 3 fritters on a dish, top with the avocado-mango sauce, and garnish with fried shallots and parsley.

To Drink with Your Meal...

Wine: The subtle flavors of this dish, along with the deep frying and the mango, will match well with a crisp, high-acid wine, such as a **Sauvignon Blanc**, **Pinot Gris**, or **Riesling**.
• Kenwood Sauvignon Blanc
• South Coast Riesling

Beer: A crisp and effervescent beer with a citrus, spicy character will work well with this dish. Try a **Saison** or **Witbier**.
• The Bruery's Saison Rue
• Coronado's Orange Ave Wit

SHRIMP MOJITO COCKTAIL WITH AVOCADO-WASABI SORBET

Serves 4 to 6 • Total time: 24+ hours / Active: 2 hours

San Diego has an event every November called the "San Diego Bay Wine and Food Festival," and it's a time when gourmands come out to play. On average, more than 4,000 people attend. My chef friends and I like to pull out all the stops and try to impress while having fun with our dishes. I created this dish with a specific theme in mind — I teamed up with my friend at Sydney Frank Imports and featured his Tommy Bahama rum. I had done ceviche many times before, but I had the idea to add the rum and some mint, which would make it more like a mojito. Aha! Then I thought: Why not do it with some sorbet to keep it cold and with a kick of wasabi? This dish won third place for the festival's Chef of the Fest contest in 2009. It was a wonderful surprise and an honor to receive such recognition for what I do.

MOJITO MARINADE

1	tablespoon	honey
¼	cup	fresh cilantro, chopped
¼	cup	vegetable or canola oil
20	leaves	fresh mint, chopped
4		limes, zest and juice
1	cup	Tommy Bahama rum
1½	pounds	shrimp, peeled and deveined (size 16/20 is best)

COCKTAIL

10	leaves	fresh mint, chopped
1	cup	Tommy Bahama rum
2		limes, zest and juice

AVOCADO-WASABI SORBET

4	tablespoons	granulated sugar
2	tablespoons	light corn syrup
1½	tablespoons	wasabi powder*
2	cups	water
¼	cup	fresh lime juice
2 to 3		medium Hass avocados, diced
¼	teaspoon	kosher salt

TOMATO SALSA

2	cups	fresh tomatoes, ½-inch dice
½	cup	red onion, ½-inch dice
1	bunch	fresh cilantro, chopped
1	teaspoon	ground cumin
½	cup	fresh lemon juice
		salt and pepper to taste

CONTINUED >

An ice bath — a bowl filled with ice and water — comes in very handy for a number of things in the kitchen. When preparing beautiful vegetables, you'll often want to blanch them in boiling water, then plunge them directly into an ice bath. Blanching the vegetables preserves their vibrant colors, and gently and quickly cooks them. The ice bath stops the cooking process.

When you're preparing a pastry crème, crème Anglaise, curd, or syrup, you want to cook the mixture until it thickens just to the proper point — but then you want to stop the cooking immediately so the residual heat doesn't overcook it. An ice bath provides the perfect way to cool the mixture fast. Simply place the hot stuff in a metal mixing bowl, lay it inside the bowl with the ice bath, and stir it to distribute the cold.

1. Make the marinade. In a medium bowl, whisk together honey, cilantro, oil, mint, rum, and lime juice and zest until well combined. Add the shrimp, coat well, and cover with plastic wrap and place in refrigerator for at least 24 hours, but no longer than 36. The shrimp should begin to look opaque and no longer raw. (This is a form of pickling, called ceviche.) Now they're ready. Drain the liquid from shrimp, and cut each into 4 equal pieces. To make the cocktail, place the cut shrimp into a clean dish with the mint, rum, lime zest, and juice.

2. Make the sorbet. In a small sauce pot, make a simple syrup: heat sugar, corn syrup, wasabi, and water and bring to a boil. Put the liquid in the refrigerator or in an ice bath *(See Chef's Tip, This Page)* to chill. In a blender, combine the simple syrup with the remaining ingredients and purée until smooth. Put into an ice cream maker and follow manufacturer's directions. Reserve for service.

3. Combine all the tomato salsa ingredients in a bowl, season with salt and pepper, and reserve for service.

4. Since it's a cocktail, you'll want to use martini glasses or other festive dishes for this. Place about 1 cup of the shrimp mojito mixture in a glass, then top with 1 tablespoon of the salsa and ¼ cup of the sorbet. Make sure to not eat and drive. Cheers!

Groves of trees at Stehly Farms Organics in Bonsall.

Milagro Farm Vineyards & Winery

Once you get about 20 minutes north of downtown San Diego, and about 20 minutes east, you're in Ramona, which is real farm country. Milagro Farm is tucked away off a dirt road — an unassuming location, until you drive through the beautiful stone entrance and onto the grounds.

When owners Kit and Karen Sickels bought this majestic 90-acre property in 2001, they knew from the start that they wanted to make their own wine. They didn't realize, though, that the incredible grape-growing potential of their place would move them to create a full-fledged winery in only a few years.

By 2006, winemaker Jim Hart had come aboard to help the Sickels take Milagro to the next level. Under Jim's direction, more acreage was planted and new varieties were introduced. Jim was truly excited by the potential he saw in this remote area of San Diego County. The decomposed granite content in the soil was ideal for vinifera grapes, and the 2,400-foot elevation made for the quicker-cooling days that most varieties love.

When Milagro released its first bottling in 2006 (Chardonnay), the reaction was overwhelmingly positive. Not only was the quality of the wine great, people couldn't believe it was made from grapes grown in Ramona. "All our wines are estate grown," Jim says, "and that's one of the things that's going to set us apart from the others." Recognition at major wine competitions will also set Milagro off from the others. In 2010, Milagro's '09 Sauvignon Blanc won a gold medal at the New World International Wine Competition, and the '07 Cabernet took silver.

All their initial success has inspired the Sickels to nearly double the number of acres under cultivation and to expand the types of wine they make. Jim showed me some recently planted areas that include Sangiovese, Cabernet Franc, Petite Syrah, and Aleatico, among others. Kit and Karen are a bit bemused by the project that started out as sort of a hobby but has blossomed into a genuinely exciting enterprise. "This isn't just a hobby anymore," Jim says with a broad smile. "We believe we can make world-class wines."

More information about Milagro Farm Vineyards & Winery is in Featured Wineries on page 203.

Below (left to right): Milagro's beautiful Tuscan-style main winery building; Jim pulls some amazing Aleatico from the barrel for Kit; Jim, Kit, and Karen at Milagro's hand-crafted entrance.

alliums

THE GENUS *ALLIUM* CONTAINS ALMOST 700 SPECIES, several of which have culinary uses and are commonly known as onions, scallions, garlic, shallots, leeks, and chives.

Onions, which originated in the Near East and Central Asia, have been cultivated for thousands of years. The most familiar is the common, or bulbous, onion, which may have a yellow, white, red, or purple skin. Many people think that scallions are a separate type of onion, but in fact they're simply the immature plants of any bulbing onion, harvested before the bulb is fully formed. Scallions may also be called spring onions, green onions, or salad onions.

A native of Central Asia, garlic historically has been prized for both culinary and medicinal uses. It has the strongest flavor of all the *alliums*. Black garlic, in particular, is gaining in popularity in the United States. It is made by fermenting whole bulbs of garlic at high temperature, a process that results in black cloves. The taste is sweet and syrupy with hints of balsamic or even tamarind.

Shallots are believed to have been brought by the Crusaders to Europe from ancient Israel. Like their garlic cousins, shallots grow as bulbs divided into cloves — usually 2, but occasionally as many as 10. Shallots grow in clusters and have a distinctive tapered shape. They are most often a copper brown color but also may be reddish or gray. Their flavor, sometimes described as a blend of sweet onion and garlic, makes them a favorite of chefs.

Leeks look like gigantic scallions and are the largest member of the *allium* family. Thought to be native to Asia and the Mediterranean, leeks have been cultivated for more than 3,000 years. Wild leeks, or ramps, are a spring delicacy and native to North America. They look like green onions with broader leaves, and have a wonderfully pungent garlic aroma.

Chives look like tall tufts of grass and are, in fact, closely related to grass. Chives can be clipped with scissors and used straight from the garden or window pot. Garlic chives, also called Chinese chives or Oriental chives, are good as a mild substitute for garlic.

CHILE-MARINATED ONION AND CAMBAZOLA BRUSCHETTA

Serves 4 • Total time: 24+ hours / Active: 40 minutes

I created this onion recipe when Terra first opened. In those days, we actually used the liquid and not the onions. I thought of the marinated onions as a "by-product" that I would toss into various salsas and salads. After a while, I realized these onions were delicious as a featured ingredient, so now they star in this recipe.

CHILE-ONION MARINADE

5	cloves	fresh garlic
5		fresh bay leaves
1	tablespoon	black peppercorns
2	teaspoons	fresh thyme, chopped
2	tablespoons	allspice berries
1	cup	white wine vinegar
1	cup	balsamic vinegar
2	cups	water
2	cups	brown sugar
4		medium red onions, 1-inch slices
2		ancho chile peppers*

CAMBAZOLA BRUSCHETTA

1		baguette or Italian bread
8	ounces	cambazola cheese (or brie or camembert), rind removed
		salt and pepper to taste

1. With the garlic, bay leaves, peppercorns, thyme, and allspice, make a sachet by tying a piece of cheesecloth into a bundle with twine. In a large stock pot combine the vinegars, water, and sugar. Add the sachet and onion, and simmer for 20 minutes. Remove from heat, add the chiles, and let the mixture sit overnight. Remove the sachet and strain, reserving the liquid and the onions separately.

2. Preheat oven to 400°F. Slice the baguette into 2-inch slices, either on a bias or straight across. Grill or toast the slices to give them a more complex flavor. For an even better flavor, brush the slices with either garlic oil or olive oil. Then season slightly with salt and pepper before toasting or grilling.

3. Place 1 tablespoon of the cooked onions on the toasted bread, top with a ½-ounce portion of cheese, and place on a baking sheet. Continue with the remaining slices of bread. Place the sheet in the oven and bake for about 5 minutes, or until the cheese is melted.

Chef's Tip: Using Onion/Chile/Vinegar Liquid. If you reduce this liquid to a syrup consistency, it makes a terrific vinaigrette when mixed with oil. I have always loved using it with olive oil as a dressing, but it will also work beautifully with almost any other type of oil, including grapeseed, canola, or hazelnut.

To Drink with Your Meal...

Wine: The spice of the chiles and the piquancy of the onions make this dish a perfect match for an Alsatian-style wine, such as a **Riesling** or a **Gewürztraminer.**
- South Coast Riesling
- Gundlach Bundschu Gewürztraminer

Beer: A hoppy American **IPA** will cut the spice from the chiles, while drawing out floral and fruity flavors from the Cambazola.
- AleSmith IPA
- Port Wipeout IPA

Orfila Vineyards & Winery

Few people know that California's multibillion-dollar wine industry traces its roots to San Diego. The mission fathers at Mission San Diego de Alcala (California's first mission) were making wine as far back as the 1700s. Despite that unique history, it wasn't all that long ago (less than 20 years) that the words "San Diego" and "wine" would never be used in the same sentence. Well, a lot has changed in the past two decades, and much of that change is credited to Orfila Winery. In many ways, Orfila made San Diego relevant again in the wine world.

Orfila Vineyards first opened in 1994, when Alejandro Orfila (a retired Argentine ambassador) bought the winery

Above: Sales Manager Scott Ledbetter walks me through the vineyard. Below: The spectacular view from just outside the tasting room. Opposite: Tasting through the Orfila wine list (yum!).

from Thomas Jaeger. Jaeger had purchased the original San Pasqual Winery, which had been making wine at that location since 1973. When the ambassador first took over, the vineyard was entirely planted to chardonnay (that was the "California craze" at the time). It wasn't long before Orfila and winemaker Leon Santoro realized that this unique property (500 feet up and less than 15 miles from the Pacific) could potentially produce a whole host of other varietals. Santoro began extensive experimentation and research. Eventually, he was convinced that varietals native to France's Rhone Valley held some of the winery's greatest potential. So, the chardonnay got pulled, and the Roussanne, Marsanne, Viognier, and Syrah got planted.

Within only a few short years, Orfila was producing some truly excellent estate-grown Rhone-style wines. The quality of the grapes coming from the property forced many in the wine world to sit up and take notice. "Leon brought an Old-World style to the New World," explains Sales Manager Scott Ledbetter. "He came from Napa, but he made it his life goal to put San Diego back on the map."

Well, fast-forward to today. More than 1,300 medals later — from both national and international wine competitions — Orfila is consistently producing top-quality Syrah, Roussanne, Marsanne, and Viognier from their 40-acres of estate vineyards. They are also making great wine from grapes grown in other top wine-making regions, including Monterey, Edna Valley, and Santa Maria. Leon Santoro is gone, but his spirit of experimentation and exploration still continues at the winery. Scott is happy to point out various locations on various hillsides where new varieties, such as Sangiovese and Montepulciano, are coming into their own. "Right now, we're just seeing how it goes," Scott explains. "It's good to keep trying new things."

Orfila remains the flagship vineyard in the region for top-quality winemaking. It continues to carry the banner for San Diego wines and has inspired many others to start up their own wine-making ventures. Today, San Diego County boasts more than 50 wineries and is one of the nation's fastest-growing wine-making areas. Orfila's new winemaker, Justin Mund, is ready to take the winery into the future. "I'm very excited to be a part of the Orfila team as the new winemaker for the 2010 vintage," Justin says. "It's a welcome challenge to maintain and improve Orfila's already stellar wines."

The winery's contribution to the region has not gone unnoticed by local government officials. In fact, September 19, 2006, was proclaimed Orfila Vineyards & Winery Day by the San Diego County Board of Supervisors. The proclamation applauded the quality of Orfila's wines, its history of innovation, its dedication to responsible and sustainable agricultural practices, and its undeniable role in getting San Diego back on the international wine map.

More information about Orfila Vineyards & Winery is in Featured Wineries on page 203.

KARL STRAUSS AMBER LAGER–BRAISED SHORT RIBS

Serves 6 • Total time: 5 hours / Active: 90 minutes

This recipe was added to the menu during the fall of 2008 as a hearty "stick to your ribs" (get it?) kind of dish. We sell about 50 pounds of short ribs a week, and, like our popular pumpkin ravioli, they simply can't be removed from the menu. In this preparation, the short ribs are fork-tender, fall-apart-on-your-plate good. On my restaurant menu, I serve the short ribs with mashed Yukon potatoes and mushroom-leek ragout, which is a perfect accompaniment for this dish. The caramelized onion grits — which I developed in 2003 as an alternative to mashed potatoes — are added here to enhance the dish and launch it "over the top."

SHORT RIBS

6	7-ounce	boneless short ribs (42 ounces total)
½	cup	kosher salt
½	cup	freshly ground black pepper
¼	cup	canola oil
1	cup	carrot, chopped
½	cup	celery, chopped
½	cup	yellow onion, chopped
6	cloves	fresh garlic
1		Granny Smith apple, quartered
1		red beet, quartered
6	12-ounce bottles	Karl Strauss Amber Lager
¼	cup	fresh thyme, chopped
¼	cup	fresh rosemary, chopped

CARAMELIZED ONION AND BRIE GRITS

2		brown onions
1	tablespoon	canola oil
8	cups	whole milk
2½	cups	quick grits
1	pound	brie cheese, rind removed and diced
1	teaspoon	kosher salt
1	teaspoon	freshly ground black pepper

MUSHROOM-LEEK RAGOUT

1	pound	mixed mushrooms (I use maitake, king trumpet, enoki)
½	pound	leeks, cut into ½ inch pieces and washed thoroughly
8	tablespoons	unsalted butter
1	teaspoon	kosher salt
½	teaspoon	freshly ground black pepper
¼	cup	dry white wine (the kind you'd actually drink)
¼	cup	truffle oil* (for garnish)
1		carrot, peeled and fried (for garnish)

CONTINUED >

1. Preheat oven to 350°F. Make sure to trim some of the fat off the short ribs before cooking — but don't take it all off. The fat adds a ton of flavor! Season each side of all the ribs with salt and pepper. In a large sauté pan on high heat, add the canola oil and sear each rib on every side until well browned *(See Chef's Tip, This Page)*. After all the ribs have been seared and are out of the pan, sauté the carrot, celery, and onion for about 5 minutes. Add garlic, apple, and beet and continue sautéing for another 2 to 3 minutes. Deglaze the pan with the beer, then pour the entire contents into a large roasting pan. Place the ribs in the beer mixture and add the thyme and rosemary. Cover with aluminum foil and bake for about 3½ hours or until fork tender. You can tell a perfectly cooked rib by putting a fork into it; if the fork slides right back out when picked up, the rib's done.

2. Caramelize the onions. *(See Jeff's Kitchen Advice, Page 19.)* When the onions are done, pour them out onto a clean cutting board and give them a rough chop through (once or twice) with your chef's knife (don't chop them too fine, because you'll leave a lot of that flavor on the cutting board instead of in the grits).

3. Make the grits. In a large sauce pot on medium heat, bring the milk to a boil and slowly whisk in the grits. Continue stirring and add the cheese and the caramelized onions. Season with salt and pepper. When the grits begin to thicken, take the pot off the heat and serve. (You can also turn the grits out onto a baking sheet and put them away in the refrigerator to cool. Once cooled, you can cut the grits into cakes and reheat them in a microwave or in a sauté pan.)

4. Make the mushroom-leek ragout. Chop the mushrooms into equal-size pieces so they will cook evenly. In a large sauté pan on high heat, place 4 tablespoons of the butter with the leeks. Stir or shake the pan so the butter melts but doesn't brown (brown butter would add a nutty taste to the dish, which could also be good). Sauté on high heat for about 1 minute and then add the mushrooms. Season with salt and pepper. Continue sautéing on high for another 2 minutes or until the mushrooms are tender, but not completely cooked. Turn the heat down to low, stir in the remaining butter and the wine to form an emulsion.

5. To plate: Place about ½ cup of the grits in the middle, top with the short ribs, place about ¼ cup of the ragout, fried carrot peels, then drizzle some truffle oil on top for a little more love.

Fresh rosemary at Suzie's Farm in San Diego.

Left to right: Executive Director Stan Miller, me, Gilberto Jimenez, Leilani Chavez, Angel Gomez, Kevin Valdez, Leslie Alvarez, and Assistant Site Director Lourdes de Jesus. The children are helping us pick and taste sweet peas.

NCCS Gardening Program

North County Community Services (NCCS) is a 40-year-old nonprofit organization in northern San Diego County. Its mission is to improve the health and well-being of individuals and families by providing programs that educate young children, support working families, feed the hungry, and ultimately create opportunities to improve the quality of life in the region.

In 2006, NCCS began installing small vegetable gardens at its child development facilities in Oceanside, Vista, and Escondido. The gardens serve as an "extended classroom experience" for children enrolled at the facilities. Kids participate in planting, watering, and harvesting vegetables from the gardens, and the food is incorporated into the meals they consume at the center.

Executive Director Stan Miller says he was lucky enough to grow up on a farm and always had a large garden that provided fresh food for his family. The gardens at the NCCS preschools provide a wonderful opportunity to teach children about food and life cycles, and they create a strong foundation for making healthy food choices.

During the summer season, NCCS grows great crops of tomatoes, squash, pumpkins, cucumbers, beans, corn, and potatoes. During the fall/winter season, they plant cabbage, broccoli, cauliflower, herbs, multiple varieties of lettuce, celery, onions, potatoes, and snow peas — all winter crops for the San Diego region.

Dubbed "Farming with Four-Year-Olds," the program provides preschool children a variety of experiences that introduce them to the fun of eating healthy, home-grown food. How many three- or four-year-olds do you know who will eat basil? How about broccoli, or raw green beans, or peas? By introducing taste tests in the classroom and involving the children in growing their own food, they not only know what they are eating, they also take great pride in eating it.

SPRING ONION RAVIOLI

Serves 4 • Total time: 90 minutes / Active: 40 minutes

When Terra first opened, we served pumpkin ravioli, and they quickly became one of our most popular items. When we took them off the menu and replaced them with this onion ravioli recipe, we had a revolt on our hands. But we eventually brought back the pumpkin ravioli because our customers kept begging for them. (See Recipe, Page 96.)

1	tablespoon	canola oil
4		spring onions, cleaned and sliced (or 1 medium red onion, sliced)
1	teaspoon	fresh thyme leaves
3		large eggs, lightly beaten with a little water (for egg wash)
40		round gyoza/potsticker wrappers *
¼	cup	cornmeal
1	cup	balsamic vinegar
2	tablespoons	unsalted butter
¼	cup	freshly grated parmesan cheese (or any other hard cheese)

1. In a sauce pan over medium heat, cook the onions in the oil until translucent, and most of the moisture has cooked off. Lower the heat to low and continue to cook until onions begin to brown. Take the pan off the heat and add the thyme.

2. Make the ravioli. Place half of the wonton wrappers on a flat surface, brush the edges lightly with the egg wash, and place 1 teaspoon of the onion mixture in the center of each. Lay another wrapper on top, removing any air pockets and ensuring that the edges are sealed. Place the ravoli on a baking sheet that is lightly dusted with cornmeal until ready to cook, or you may freeze them at this point. (Freeze the ravioli in single layers so they don't stick together.)

3. There are two ways to cook the ravioli: 1. The traditional way is in boiling water for 1½ minutes if the ravioli are already at room temperature, or for 2½ minutes if they're taken from the freezer. 2. The alternate way is to sauté the ravioli in 2 tablespoons of canola oil for about 1 minute on each side.

4. If boiling the ravioli, take a medium sauté pan and melt butter over moderate heat and slowly add the balsamic vinegar while whisking rapidly. This will combine, or emulsify, the ingredients to create the sauce. Then add the ravioli to the sauce to coat. If sautéing the ravioli, place the butter and balsamic in the pan just after the ravioli have been seared and removed, then emulsify to make the sauce. Turn out onto a clean plate with the sauce and dust with freshly grated parmesan cheese or serve with a cheese crisp. To make the crisps, sprinkle enough grated cheese to thinly cover a 3-inch diameter circle on a parchment-lined baking sheet. Bake at 400°F for 2 to 3 minutes.

> **Chef's Tip: Heating Ravioli.** If you're making more than 1 panful of ravioli, turn out the completed ravioli onto a baking sheet with a little of the sauce. When you've finished sautéing all the ravioli, place the baking sheet in the oven to reheat. Then place 2, 3, or 4 ravioli (whatever your portion) into a bowl or onto a plate, top with sauce and cheese, and serve.

GRILLED CHEESE "TOAST" WITH MUSHROOMS AND ROASTED SHALLOTS

Serves 4 to 6 • Total time: 50 minutes / Active: 25 minutes

Who doesn't like bread? — especially when you add cheese, mushrooms, and shallots! Shallots have a lighter complexity than red onions, but when roasted, they have an amazing depth of caramelized and sweetened flavor. You can substitute any of your favorite mushrooms in this recipe — just make sure you don't over sauté them, since you'll also be baking them with the toast to melt the cheese. This is one simple dish where I urge you to take the time to grill the sliced bread for another layer of flavor. I'm all about layers of flavor, and about tempting your taste buds with each bite. If you can use roasted garlic oil here, that would give you an even better, more complex flavor.

12		shallots
¾	cup	olive oil
		salt and pepper
½	pound	mixed mushrooms (I use morel, maitake, shiitake, king oyster)
1	tablespoon	fresh garlic, minced
2	tablespoons	red wine
2	teaspoons	fresh thyme, chopped
1		baguette
10	ounces	brie cheese, rind removed and diced

1. Preheat oven to 450°F.

2. Cut the shallots into equal-size pieces (halved or in thirds). Place the shallots in a small bowl, toss them with ¼ cup of the oil, salt and pepper, and turn out onto a baking sheet. Bake the shallots for about 30 minutes, or until tender and slightly caramelized.

3. On a clean cutting board, cut all the mushrooms into 2- to 3- inch, equal-size pieces. Put ¼ cup of oil in a medium sauté pan on medium-high heat and sauté the mushrooms. Season the mushrooms with a pinch of salt and pepper, and turn the heat down to medium low. Add the garlic, wine, and half the thyme. Continue to sauté for another minute, or until the wine has evaporated. Take off the heat and reserve.

4. Slice the baguette into equal slices. With a pastry brush, slather each slice of bread with the remaining olive oil and season with salt and pepper. Grill the slices on each side or toast them in a toaster oven or in the oven.

5. Slice the brie into equal-size pieces.

6. Place 1 tablespoon of the mushroom mixture and a piece of brie on each slice of bread. Top each with 1 or 2 wedges of roasted shallot. Continue with all the bread slices and place in the oven for about 5 minutes, or until the cheese is melted.

7. Garnish with remaining thyme.

To Drink with Your Meal...

Wine: The simple grilled and roasted flavors of this dish, along with the cheese, enable it to pair nicely with either a white or a red wine. If you're in the mood for white, a **Sauvignon Blanc** would work perfectly. If you're a red fan, try a **Pinot Noir**, or a lighter, fruitier **Sangiovese**.

• Hart Sauvignon Blanc
• Sanford Pinot Noir

Beer: The cheese and roasted shallots make a wonderful pairing with any beer with an earthy, hops character, such as an **ESB** or **Strong Pale Ale**.

• Fuller's ESB
• Double Dog Pale Ale

LOBSTER TAMAL WITH QUINOA, LEEKS, AND CORN

Serves 6 • Total time: 90 minutes / Active: 45 minutes

Technically speaking, this dish is misnamed. It's actually a quinoa tamal, since the quinoa — not the lobster — is wrapped in the banana leaf. But, for the menu at Terra, it's much more appealing to say "lobster tamal." A tamal is a Central American version of the Mexican tamale, but it uses banana leaves instead of corn husks. Quinoa is originally from Peru and is known as the "super grain." Quinoa is a complete protein source and, contrary to popular opinion, it is a seed and not a grain.

6	cups	water
2	teaspoons	kosher salt
2	cups	quinoa (any color)
1	tablespoon	canola oil
¼	cup	yellow onion, small dice
½	cup	carrot, small dice
2	tablespoons	fresh oregano, chopped
1	teaspoon	freshly ground black pepper
1	package	frozen banana leaves*
6	tablespoons	unsalted butter
3	cups	leeks, julienned, whites only
1	pound	cooked lobster meat
1	cup	fresh corn, sliced off the cob
1	tablespoon	water

1. Bring 6 cups of water and 1 teaspoon of kosher salt to a boil. Stir the quinoa into the boiling water and boil for 5 to 7 minutes until tender. Strain the quinoa and rinse with cold water to stop the cooking process. Set aside in a bowl.

2. In a very hot sauté pan, add the canola oil and coat the pan well. Add the onion, carrot, oregano, pepper, and ½ teaspoon salt and sauté until slightly caramelized. Pour the mixture into the quinoa and mix until thoroughly combined.

3. To assemble: banana leaves must be at room temperature. Remove the center rib from the leaves and cut along the grain into approximately 7-inch-wide pieces. Save some pieces to use as ties for the packages. Heat each piece on both sides over a flame for about 15 seconds to make the leaves more pliable. Put 1 cup of quinoa mixture into the center of each leaf and fold the sides over the grain to make a package. Bunch one open end of the package and tie it with a strip of the reserved banana leaf pieces, then fold the other end underneath.

4. Tamals can be kept refrigerated for up to 4 days. When ready to use, the easiest method of heating is wrapping the packages in either plastic wrap or in plastic bags and then placing them in a microwave for about 1 minute each. Alternatively, you can either set up a steamer and steam the packages for 20 minutes, or you can put the packages in the oven for approximately 7 minutes at 350°F.

5. To finish the tamals: melt the butter in a medium sauté pan over medium heat until the butter begins to foam. Add the leeks and cook until tender. Add the lobster and corn and just warm through. DO NOT OVERCOOK! Add water to the sauté pan and whisk to emulsify. Add remaining salt and pepper and remove from heat.

6. To plate: Take a hot tamal, slice the top, and unfold. Spoon the lobster mixture with sauce over each and serve.

RAMPS, MOREL MUSHROOMS, AND MIXED GREENS

Serves 6 • Total time: 25 minutes / Active: 25 minutes

This is a simple yet underutilized way to cook and eat vegetables. These particular products are spring vegetables, but depending on what part of the country you're from, they may be available at other times as well. Ramps are also known as wild leeks — they look like overgrown green onions, but the green tops are milder in flavor. I chop about half of the green leaves separately, air-dry them for a few hours then freeze them in an air-tight container for future use as a seasoning. Feel free to substitute any other favorite mushrooms in place of the morels. This recipe is very similar to the mushroom-leek ragout in the short rib recipe. This is a technique as well as a recipe so just let your mind wander and see how you like this. This mixture can be used in omelets, with potatoes, simply eaten as a side, or even chopped up and used on a bruschetta.

1	pound	morel mushrooms
8	tablespoons	unsalted butter
½	pound	whole ramps, washed
½	pound	mixed greens (I use chard, kale, beet greens, mustard greens)
1	teaspoon	kosher salt
½	teaspoon	freshly ground black pepper
¼	cup	white wine (the kind you'd drink)

1. Chop the mushrooms into equal-size pieces so they cook evenly. Set aside.

2. In a large sauté pan on high heat, add 4 tablespoons of the butter and sauté the ramps and mixed greens. Stir or shake the pan so the butter melts but doesn't brown. Sauté on medium heat for about 2 minutes and then add the mushrooms. Season with salt and pepper. Continue cooking on medium heat for another 2 minutes, or until the mushrooms are tender, but not completely cooked. With a slotted spoon, remove the vegetables from the pan and reserve in a bowl.

3. Turn the heat down to low. Add the remaining butter and wine and emulsify to make the sauce.

4. To plate: Spoon the vegetable mix into the center and top with sauce.

To Drink with Your Meal...

Wine: This relatively light dish pairs well with a lighter style wine, such as a **Pinot Gris, Rosé** or a steely, minerally **Sauvignon Blanc**.
- Fallbrook Sauvignon Blanc Reserve
- Sofia Rosé

Beer: Light and refreshing is the way to go with this dish — try a **Light Lager** or a **Pilsner**.
- Oskar Blues Yella Pils
- Karl Strauss Endless Summer Light

tomatoes

BELIEVED TO HAVE ORIGINATED in the Andes Mountains of South America about 2,000 years ago, tomatoes were taken around the world by Spanish explorers, who brought them back to Europe in the 1500s. They have been considered poisonous — because of their strong odor and bright red and yellow "berries" — and also an aphrodisiac — they were called "love apples" by the Italians. Tomatoes did not take root in North America until the 1700s, when Thomas Jefferson tasted them in Paris and sent seeds back to America to grow on his Virginia farm.

Botanically speaking, tomatoes are fruits, not vegetables. There are around 7,500 varieties — heirlooms, in particular, are becoming very popular among gardeners and organic producers. Tomatoes come in all different sizes – grape, cherry, small, medium, and large — and shapes — including pear, heart, elongated, ruffle tops, ridges, and plums. Tomatoes are also quite colorful. In addition to red, there are yellow, orange, black, purple, pink, green, white, and striped varieties.

As a chef, I find working with tomatoes to be both challenging and satisfying. Every kind of tomato has its own unique make-up. Some are juicy, others are meaty; some are sweet, others are tart. Tomatoes also vary wildly according to when they were picked, what the growing season was like, and, of course, where they were grown. This makes writing recipes for tomatoes sort of a gamble — it's a good bet that the tomatoes you use will be completely different from the ones I used. So, the key here is: Use your senses. That means check, taste, and season as you go. In some cases you may need to add a little sugar or more salt. In other cases, you may need to adjust the cooking time, depending on the moisture content of the tomatoes you're using.

There are few edibles more satisfying than fresh, ripe, beautiful tomatoes right off the vine. The cool thing is that almost anyone can find fresh tomatoes — get them from your local organic farms, Farmers' Markets, or grow them yourself in a pot on your patio or balcony.

HEIRLOOM CHERRY TOMATO FETTUCCINI

Serves 4 • Total time: 90 minutes / Active: 60 minutes

This is a very simple, classic pasta that is all about technique. When I went back to Boston for a week in 1997 and worked at Café Louis, the sous chef made this for an employee meal one night that I'll never forget. He showed me his secret: This pasta uses cherry or grape tomatoes that need some time in the pan in order to burst open and release their goodness — so they need to go in first. Once the tomatoes open, add the garlic and the basil and watch carefully, making sure they don't brown or overcook. Remember, cooking is about technique!

¾	cup	olive oil or roasted garlic oil
1	pound	heirloom cherry or grape tomatoes
1	cup	fresh basil, loosely packed
10	cloves	fresh garlic, mashed and minced
½	teaspoon	kosher salt
¼	teaspoon	freshly ground black pepper
1½	pounds	freshly made basil fettuccini *(See Pasta Dough Recipe, Page 19)*
1 to 2	gallons	water
½	cup	arugula
½	cup	freshly grated asiago (or any aged gouda, parmesan, or gruyère)

1. In a large sauté pan, heat the olive oil on medium heat and add the tomatoes. Sauté for about 3 to 4 minutes, or until the tomatoes begin to soften, burst, or even break apart.

2. Chiffonade the basil.

3. Add the garlic, basil, salt and pepper to the tomatoes and continue to sauté for about another minute.

4. Cook the pasta in boiling water, drain, then add to the sauté pan. Add the arugula and cheese, toss until well coated, and spoon into a bowl to serve.

Chef's Tip: To Salt and Oil, or Not? Some issues seem to split the culinary world down the middle; such is the nature of what you do to water for cooking pasta. One camp, call them the "traditionalists," insists that the water should be plain and unadulterated. The other camp, call them the "seasoners," insists that pasta water should be salted and/or oiled before coming to a boil. The answer: It all depends on your preference. Either way works, and — of course — the jury is still out on which technique is really "better." Oil in the water? All that does is keep your sauce, whatever it may be, away from your pasta. Ideally, you pull the pasta from the water when it's JUST underdone and finish it in the sauce. Either way, you want the pasta to absorb just a bit of the sauce. It makes all the difference in the world — and if your pasta is coated with oil, it doesn't happen.

To Drink with Your Meal...

Wine: The garlic and asiago cheese give this dish some bold flavors without heaviness. A full-bodied white, such as a **Chardonnay** or an oak-aged **Sauvignon Blanc** would work beautifully.
- Orfila Ambassador's Reserve Chardonnay
- Groth Sauvignon Blanc

Beer: A crisp, dry, and effervescent beer will refresh the palate of assertive flavors between bites.
- Lost Abbey Avant Garde
- Saison Dupont

Wine: The acidity and freshness of this cold dish pairs well with a light, crisp, and cold white, such as a **Roussanne** or even a floral **California Rosé** (which is not White Zinfandel!).
- Hart Roussanne
- Fallbrook Rosato Sangiovese Rosé

Beer: This dish is light and refreshing, so stay with a light and refreshing **Pilsner** or **Kolsch**.
- Sierra Nevada Summerfest
- Alaskan Summer

HEIRLOOM TOMATO AND CUCUMBER SALAD

Serves 6 to 8 • Total time: 30 minutes / Active: 30 minutes

This salad is very simple yet sophisticated. Much like its cousin, the gazpacho, this salad features fresh tomatoes that can vary in acidity and sugar content from tomato to tomato. Sometimes tomatoes picked from the same vine have differences. That's why it's so important to use your senses and adjust salt, sugar, or acid (such as lemon) as you go. This salad is a rendition of an Israeli or Persian salad by the same name. In my kosher catering division we make this recipe a lot. It's meant to be a condiment on falafel with a little hummus and hot sauce, but I love this salad in the summer or early fall when tomatoes are at their peak. You also can add some bell pepper; just make sure to chop the onion and peppers small so they don't overpower the tomato and cucumber flavors.

1	pound	Persian cucumbers (or English or other type)
2	pounds	grape heirloom tomatoes (or any type of heirloom)
1/4	pound	red pearl onions
1		lemon, juiced
1	teaspoon	kosher salt
1/4	teaspoon	freshly ground black pepper
2	tablespoons	extra virgin olive oil
1/4	teaspoon	ground cumin
1/4	teaspoon	garlic powder
1/2	cup	mint leaves, chiffonade or whole

1. Cut the cucumber into slices. Cut the pearl onions in half.

2. If using pear, teardrop or cherry tomatoes, cut the tomatoes in half. If using full-size tomatoes, make tomato petals. *(See Chef's Tip, Below)*

3. In a bowl, combine all the ingredients, except the mint, and toss. Garnish with mint.

Note: Any recipe that is not cooked, including this raw salad, develops more flavor after it sits for a day or so. This recipe can be made and kept for up to 3 days. Items that sit too long can become "flat" and lose some of their flavor. They may need to be "refreshed" with salt, pepper, or a little acid.

> **Chef's Tip: Making Tomato Petals.** On a cutting board, lay tomato pieces skin-side down and, taking a sharp knife, run the blade along the skin and cut out the pulp, making tomato petals. Make sure to leave enough "meat" on the skin (about 1/4 inch). Reserve the tomato pulp to purée with the other vegetable scraps. Lay the "petals" down and cut them into 1- to 2-inch equal-size pieces.

TOMATO GAZPACHO

Serves 6 to 8 • Total time: 40 minutes / Active: 40 minutes

This soup is very simple. Still, you'll definitely need to use your senses to determine if this soup needs more salt or acid. I originally developed this recipe for a Share Our Strength event at Loews Coronado Bay Resort and paired it with a lime sorbet. Longtime Terra fans Jon and Susan Huberman ask for this all the time.

GAZPACHO

4		assorted large heirloom tomatoes
1		pasilla pepper
1		yellow bell pepper
1		red bell pepper
1		English or heirloom cucumber
1/2		red onion
4	cloves	fresh garlic
1/2	bunch	fresh cilantro, chopped
1/4	cup	fresh mint, chopped
1		lemon, juiced
1/2	teaspoon	tabasco
2	tablespoons	extra virgin olive oil
2	teaspoons	kosher salt
1	teaspoon	freshly ground black pepper
		fresh micro chives (for garnish)

LIME SORBET (SUGGESTED SIDE DISH, NOT PICTURED)

8		limes, juiced, reserve emptied halves
2	cups	simple syrup *(See Recipe, Page 19)*
1	cup	water

1. Slice tomatoes open, cut the flesh out and reserve it to purée later. Make tomato petals. *(See Chef's Tip, Page 72.)* Cut the petals into 1/2-inch dice. Reserve for service.

2. Cut the tops and bottoms off of the pasilla, and yellow and red bell peppers and reserve them to purée later. Slice the peppers open and lay them on their skins. Carefully slice off the inside ribs of the peppers and reserve them to purée later. Take 1/4 of the peppers (the remaining 3/4 peppers can be added to the purée), lay them open and slice into julienne strips. Turn the slices 90 degrees and cut the slices into 1/2-inch dice. Reserve for service.

3. Cut 1/4 of the cucumber into lengthwise strips and then cut into 1/2-inch dice (the remaining 3/4 cucumber can be added to the purée). In a bowl, combine the diced cucumbers, tomatoes and peppers.

4. Take all of the vegetables for purée and place them into a blender with the remaining ingredients. Purée until everything is combined and then pour into a bowl. Taste and adjust seasoning, if necessary.

5. At this point, ladle the gazpacho into individual bowls and garnish with the reserved diced vegetables, and micro chives. Lime sorbet (not pictured) makes another great garnish. To add that, go to step 6.

6. Make the lime sorbet. Discard membranes from empty lime halves. Place them on a baking sheet and freeze while making the sorbet. In a bowl, stir together 1 cup of the lime juice, syrup, and water, then freeze in an ice cream maker.

7. Place a scoop of sorbet in a frozen lime half and serve on the side with the soup, or just put the scoop of sorbet on top of the soup to keep the soup extra cold.

To Drink with Your Meal...

Wine: The acidity and crispness of this cold soup pairs well with a light, crisp, and cold white, such as a **Pinot Gris** or a grassy **Sauvignon Blanc**. If you add the lime sorbet, you may want a wine with a little sweetness, such as a **Riesling**.

- Milagro Farm Sauvignon Blanc
- Navarro Riesling

Beer: This dish is light and refreshing, so stick with a light and refreshing **Witbier**.

- New Belgium Sunshine Wheat
- Samuel Adams White

CURRIED PASTA SALAD WITH TOMATOES AND GOLDEN RAISINS

Serves 6 to 8 • Total time: 45 minutes / Active: 45 minutes

One of my cooks came up with this recipe for one of the Barbecue and Blues nights we do during the summers at the restaurant. The dish was originally conceived as a side — a delicious way to utilize a bunch of fresh ingredients we often had left over on Mondays, after our big Sunday brunch push. It became so popular that, now, many of my customers come in on a regular basis just to buy it by the quart!

PASTA

1 to 2	gallons	water
1	pound	bowtie pasta
¼	cup	celery, ½-inch dice
¼	cup	golden raisins
¼	cup	red onion, ½-inch dice
1	cup	tomatoes, ½-inch dice or teardrops, cut in half
⅛	cup	fresh cilantro, chopped
¼	teaspoon	kosher salt
¼	teaspoon	freshly ground black pepper

CURRY DRESSING

1½	cups	mayonnaise
1½	tablespoons	curry powder, preferably Madras
1	teaspoon	kosher salt
1	teaspoon	freshly ground black pepper
½	cup	honey

1. In a medium stock pot, bring the water to a boil, add the pasta, and cook for about 8 minutes until fully cooked. *(See Chef's Tip: To Salt and Oil, or Not?, Page 71.)* Usually, pasta should be cooked *al dente*, which still has a firmness, but this is a pasta salad so the pasta needs to be fully cooked. Put ice in the pot to cool the pasta down quickly, and then strain.

2. While waiting for the pasta to cook and then cool, whisk together all ingredients for the dressing in a medium bowl.

3. In the bowl with the dressing, add the pasta with the rest of the ingredients and combine thoroughly. You can serve this right away or let the flavors all blend together for an hour or so first.

HEIRLOOM TOMATO PIZZA

Yields 6 individual pizzas • Total time: 90 minutes / Active: 60 minutes

When we first opened Terra, we offered a grilled pizza as a starter called "An American Pie." It had smoked tomatoes and fresh mozzarella. Now, I love to use the smoker for just about anything. If you have some extra time, crack open a bottle of wine, fire up the smoker, and put a little smoke on your tomatoes first. Pizzas are so universal that any farm fresh produce can be used. This pizza calls for fresh mozzarella cheese, but feel free to try gruyère, aged gouda, parmesan, asiago, or any other cheese that tickles your fancy.

PIZZA DOUGH

4½	cups	whole wheat flour
1¾	teaspoons	salt
1	teaspoon	instant yeast
¼	cup	olive oil
1¾	cups	water, ice cold
3	tablespoons	fresh herbs, chopped (optional)
		semolina flour or cornmeal (for dusting)
¼	cup	extra virgin olive oil or roasted garlic oil (for brushing pizzas)

TOPPING

6		small red onions
6		assorted medium heirloom tomatoes
24	ounces	fresh mozzarella cheese
6	tablespoons	fresh basil, whole leaves or chopped

1. Stir together the flour, salt, and instant yeast in the bowl of an electric mixer. By hand, stir in the oil and the cold water until all is absorbed. Add the herbs. Then using the dough hook, mix on medium speed for 5 to 7 minutes, or as long as it takes to create a smooth, sticky dough. The dough should clear the sides of the bowl but stick to the bottom of the bowl (to me it looks like a tornado). Add a touch of water or flour to reach the desired consistency. The finished dough will be springy, elastic, and sticky, not just tacky.

2. Transfer the dough to a floured, flat surface, cut it into 6 equal pieces, and mold each piece into a ball. Rub each ball with olive oil, place on a well-oiled baking sheet, wrap in plastic and let proof for about 30 minutes.

3. When you are ready to make the pizza, unwrap the dough balls and dust with flour. Working one at a time, gently press a dough ball into a disk wide enough that you can bring it up onto your knuckles to thin it out — you should be able to pull (or roll with a rolling pin) each ball out to 12 inches or so. If the dough is being fussy and keeps springing back, let it rest for another 15 to 20 minutes. Place the pulled-out dough on a cornmeal-dusted baking sheet, and jerk the pan to make sure the dough will move around on the cornmeal (you don't want it to stick to the pan).

4. Preheat your grill. Slice the red onions into 1-inch slices, lightly brush the slices with oil, and grill them for about 5 minutes on each side. Reserve the slices for the top of the pizza. Slice the tomatoes into ½-inch slices, and brush them with oil.

5. Brush the pizza dough with oil, season with salt and pepper, and begin grilling the first side. When the first side is ready, flip the dough, add the sliced onion, 5 to 6 slices of tomato, about 4 ounces of cheese, and about 1 tablespoon of basil on each pizza. Close the lid for about 30 seconds. Open and continue to check the pizza bottom to make sure it doesn't burn. Happy eating!

CONTINUED >

To Drink with Your Meal...

Wine: The flavors and composition of this dish are so simple and straightforward, you could drink almost any kind of light to full-bodied wine with it. If you like lighter styles, try a **Rosé** or even a **Sparkling Blanc de Blanc**. If you're a red fan, go with a fruit-forward wine, such as a **Sangiovese** or **Zinfandel**.
- Orfila Estate Rosé of Syrah
- Seghesio Family Zinfandel

Beer: The smokiness of this dish will match nicely with the smoked character of a traditional German **Rauchbier**.
- Aecht Schlenkerla Rauchbier

Chef's Tip: Controlling Grill Temperature. Controlling the temperature of the grill is key to your success. I wish you luck. When using a gas grill, the lid is your friend. Use the lid to control the heat, and to get the hot air circulating all the way around the dough. If you need your toppings to cook/melt more quickly, slap the lid on for a bit. Keep in mind, you have to be particularly vigilant with pizzas, especially those with a thin crust — they'll burn through in a flash. Broadly speaking, whatever type of outdoor oven/grill you're using, check the bottom and top of the dough, and let it tell you what it needs — more time, more heat, a flip, whatever. Be organized: Once you throw that dough onto the grill, the next steps come in rapid succession whether you're ready or not. If you've never grilled pizzas before, give it a go, but don't be upset if the first one or two aren't perfect. It's fun for a small crowd because everyone can take a turn making their own customized pizza.

Be Wise Ranch

I was really excited to have an opportunity to visit Be Wise Ranch. It's one of Southern California's premier mid-sized certified organic family farms, and it's only about half an hour away from the restaurant. Nestled in the Santa Fe and San Pasqual valleys — just 8 miles east of the Pacific Ocean — Be Wise enjoys a unique microclimate that enables it to harvest delicious, farm-fresh produce all year round.

When we arrived, we were met by Sandra Grivas Broussard, the director of operations and sales. It was obvious that she was excited to do the "grand tour" because she loves showing off the farm and its 150-plus gorgeous acres.

Sandra explained that when owners and founders Bill and Marsanne Brammer first started farming their 20 acres in northern San Diego County in 1977, the "organic food movement" was still in its infancy. The Brammers were sort of SoCal "pioneers" back then — part of a grassroots initiative led by small family growers who were committed to reducing the impact of toxic chemicals on humans, animals, and the environment.

By the 1990s, Be Wise's business was booming, but the growth in production meant they were selling more to wholesalers and less directly to individuals. Bill and his team strongly believed in remaining part of the local community, so Be Wise started a CSA (community supported agriculture) program, whereby local residents could subscribe to the farm as members and receive weekly boxes of produce delivered straight from the farm. Depending on the season, the boxes contain a dazzling variety of root vegetables, lettuces, heirloom tomatoes, strawberries, apples, citrus, melons, herbs, chard, kale, spinach, collards, zucchini, cucumbers, and more. The CSA has become a huge success and today boasts nearly 2,300 members.

The farm's organic heirloom and slicing tomatoes, strawberries, cucumbers, and zucchini also can be found at many national locations, including Jimbo's, Whole Foods, and Trader Joe's. Despite their size and success, the folks at Be Wise never lose sight of their humble beginnings. "We always keep in mind that it's our individual CSA members that form the core of who and what we are," Sandra said as we neared the end of our visit. "Our members are the reason we're here and the reason we're inspired to grow the best organic produce we can grow."

More information about Be Wise Ranch is in Featured Organic Farms on page 202.

Left to right: Strawberries in the summer sun; me with SoCal organic pioneer Bill Brammer; fields of greens; a bounty of cabbage.

Wine: The smokiness of the
grilled beef and the chipotle
make this a great dish for a
rich, smoky **Syrah** or a full-
bodied **Merlot**.
- Robert Sinskey Merlot
- Orfila Estate Syrah

Beer: The fruity and spicy
elements of the dish make it
the perfect candidate for a
Belgian-style **IPA**.
- Stone Cali-Belgique
- Green Flash Le Freak

CHIPOTLE SKIRT STEAK WITH FIRE-ROASTED TOMATO SAUCE

Serves 6 • Total time: 24+ hours / Active: 45 minutes

One of my best grill cooks, Brian Ridge, came up with this chipotle marinade for the steak. In the Terra kitchen, it was known for the longest time as "Brian's marinade." We had a rendition of this dish on the menu that was served with black beans and salsa fresca. The marinade can be made ahead of time and stored in the refrigerator for up to 1 month, and the sauce also can be made ahead of time and stored for about 1 week.

CHIPOTLE MARINADE

3		chipotle chiles with adobo sauce*
1	bunch	fresh cilantro
1	6-ounce can	tomato paste
¼	cup	fresh lime juice
2	cups	fresh orange juice
½	cup	brown sugar
2	tablespoons	honey
½	teaspoon	kosher salt
10	cloves	fresh garlic

STEAK

4	pounds	skirt steak (or flat iron, flank, or tri-tip)

FIRE-ROASTED TOMATO SAUCE

8		large tomatoes
1		medium brown onion, cut into quarters
1	cup	fresh garlic, roasted
1	bunch	fresh cilantro
1½	tablespoons	balsamic vinegar
¼	teaspoon	kosher salt
¼	teaspoon	freshly ground black pepper

1. Make the marinade. Purée all the ingredients in a blender until smooth. Put the steak in a large bowl and cover with the marinade. Cover and refrigerate for at least 24 hours and up to 48 hours.

2. Make the fire-roasted tomato sauce. On a grill, open flame, or in a 500°F oven, burn the outside of the tomatoes and the onion. When onions cook, the layers begin to peel off. Keep peeling the layers and cooking the rest. Put the charred onion and tomato into a medium sauce pot with the garlic, cilantro, and balsamic vinegar and heat thoroughly on low. Purée in a blender until smooth and season with salt, pepper, and a pinch of sugar (if needed).

3. Grill the steak to desired doneness, slice, and serve with fire-roasted tomato sauce.

VANILLA BUTTER LOBSTER WITH TOMATO CONFIT AND LOBSTER SPAETZLE

Serves 4 • Total time: 24+ hours / Active: 90 minutes

The California spiny lobster season opens around the first of October and runs through the middle of March. This recipe was created back in 2002 after teaching a cooking class and wanting to feature local items. (Maine lobster can easily be substituted in this recipe, though.) I do the vanilla butter poached lobster at times throughout the year at Terra. I've always done gnocchi and pasta but never spaetzle. I love the various microgreens available, and I got dandelion vinegar from one of my purveyors awhile ago and use it a lot as a finishing drizzle on fish. However, I tried it one Valentine's Day as a drizzle on salads and it was awesome. The tomatoes give this dish a little more acidity and balance out the lobster and the dandelion vinegar.

TOMATO CONFIT

10		medium heirloom tomatoes
¼	cup	extra virgin olive oil
4	sprigs	fresh thyme
		salt to taste

SPAETZLE

8	cups	lobster stock *(See Chef's Tip, Page 86)*
4	ounces	uncooked lobster meat
2	cloves	fresh garlic, roasted
1	teaspoon	fresh tarragon, chopped
1	teaspoon	fresh basil, chopped
1	teaspoon	brandy
2	teaspoons	heavy whipping cream
1		egg
3	tablespoons	all-purpose flour
		salt and pepper to taste

VANILLA BUTTER LOBSTER

4	cups	unsalted butter
3		vanilla beans, preferably Tahitian
2	sprigs	fresh thyme
4		uncooked lobster tails, shelled
2	cups	microgreens
2	teaspoons	truffle oil*
2	teaspoons	dandelion vinegar* (or any white infused gourmet vinegar)
		salt and pepper to taste

1. Make the tomato confit. Preheat oven to 300°F. Make an "X" on the bottom of each tomato and blanch in boiling water for about 2 minutes and then transfer to an ice bath *(See Chef's Tip, Page 44)*. Peel tomatoes, cut into quarters and make tomato petals *(See Chef's Tip, Page 72)*. Place on a baking sheet, drizzle with oil and thyme, season with salt, and bake for about 2 hours, until just before they start to caramelize and turn brown. Cool, finely dice, and reserve for service. This can be done up to a day ahead of time.

CONTINUED >

People have debated forever about the best way to kill or cook a lobster. Truth is, in the professional kitchen, the most expedient way is the best way — but that's not always the preferred way for the home cook. Some people swear by the "knife to the head" method — that is splitting open the lobster's head with a sharp knife. Others simply twist off the head and tail. Still others are loyal to the boiling water method — take the live lobster and throw it in. The truth is, all of these methods end in the same result — a cooked lobster. It's really all a matter of preference and what you are comfortable with. Of course — if you really don't want any part of it, you can always buy lobsters already boiled from your local fish store or supermarket, or just come to Terra for dinner!

To make lobster stock: After removing all the meat from a cooked lobster, wash the body cavity, and place all body parts and shells in a 400°F oven for 15 to 20 minutes. Put the roasted shells in water to cover, add mirepoix (*See Jeff's Kitchen Advice, Page 18*), fennel and tarragon can be added as well. Bring to a boil and lower to a simmer for about 1 hour. Strain and reserve.

2. Make the spaetzle. Heat stock in a medium sauce pot on medium heat until simmering. Meanwhile, place the lobster meat, remaining ingredients, and a pinch of salt and pepper in a food processor and purée until everything is combined. Let the dough rest for 10 to 15 minutes. Place in a piping bag and squeeze ½-inch drops into the hot lobster stock. Alternatively, hold a large-holed colander or slotted spoon over the simmering stock and push the dough through the holes with a spatula or spoon. Poach for about 2 to 3 minutes. Keep warm for service.

3. Prepare the lobster. In a medium sauce pot over low heat, melt the butter. Add the vanilla beans and thyme, and heat for 2 minutes. Add the lobster tails and cook until the lobster is opaque, about 12 to 15 minutes. Remove lobsters and reserve for service.

4. To plate: In a bowl, mix microgreens, truffle oil and dandelion vinegar with a pinch of salt and pepper. Spoon the hot spaetzle in the middle of a plate and then top with a generous amount of reheated tomato mixture. Top with hot poached lobster and garnish with microgreens.

Fresh tarragon at Suzie's Farm in San Diego.

Hart Winery

A lot of people in the Temecula and San Diego wine business refer to Joe Hart as "a legend" in the region's wine-making industry. That's probably because Joe's been making wine on his property in Temecula for more than 30 years. He bought the property in 1973, planted grapes a year later, and by 1980, Hart Winery celebrated its first crush. "We were the fifth winery here," Joe remembers. "We came shortly after John Moramarco from Brookside Vineyard and Winery (later from Callaway) planted the first vines."

Joe recalls looking for potential grape-growing land all over Southern California. He learned that Temecula has a nearly perfect climate for growing grapes because it's moderately warm with an ocean influence that cools things down quickly in the evening. "Climate is the number one factor in growing good grapes," Joe says. "Soils are secondary." The Hart vineyard is made up primarily of decomposed granite soil that sits about 1,500 feet above sea level. When the sun goes down, the temperature drops quickly — a chill-down that wine grapes love.

In all, Joe grows about 30 tons of grapes on his 10-acre property, and he also buys top-quality grapes from the same Temecula growers each year. All together, he makes about 15 different wines. (He confessed to me that he likes to try a little bit of everything!) Currently, he produces Sauvignon Blanc, Roussanne, Sangiovese, Barbera, Zinfandel, Syrah, Merlot, Cabernet Franc, Mourvèdre, Cabernet Sauvignon, Syrah Port, Aleatico dessert wine (it's incredible!), as well as some proprietary blends.

It's obvious that Joe is proud to be known as one of Temecula's original wine "pioneers." He's quick to remind visitors that Hart is the oldest family-owned winery in the valley, but when you ask him if he likes being called a "legend," he answers in his typically unassuming and humble way. "I guess 'legend' is okay. I don't really mind being a legend."

More information about Hart Winery is in Featured Wineries on page 203.

Left to right: At Hart, you taste wine among the rows of oak barrels that house the upcoming releases; Temecula wine-making pioneer, Joe Hart.

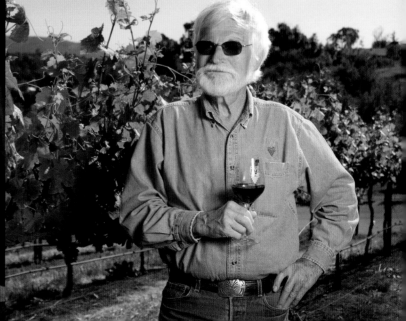

vines

OKAY, SO HERE'S WHERE ALL OUR CHAPTER CLASSIFICATIONS COLLIDE — and things get messy. Technically and botanically speaking, the vine foods we include in this chapter are fruits; we call many of them "vegetables," however, because they have relatively lower sugar levels. The fruits that we commonly call vegetables for culinary purposes include the gourdlike plants — such as cucumbers, pumpkins, squashes, okra, and eggplant — and also the legumes — such as garden peas, snap peas, soybeans, lima beans, bush beans, and pole beans. Of course, tomatoes and avocados are technically fruits as well, but we cover them separately in other chapters.

The vine-growing vegetables encompass such a wide range of plants and characteristics that we can't cover them all in detail here (just going through the four major kinds of squashes would take an entire page). Suffice it to say that California — which is the nation's largest agricultural producer — offers a huge variety of vine vegetables during all times of the year. Unlike other states, California has within its borders almost every kind of growing region, climate, and microclimate, so diversity and choice are givens. I encourage you to explore the local farms and organic producers of your immediate area, find out what they grow and when, then purchase and cook accordingly.

I hope the recipes in this section will inspire you — not only to feature these wonderfully versatile ingredients in what you cook — but also to experiment with them in your own unique and creative way.

PUMPKIN BISQUE WITH CINNAMON CREMA

Yields 4 quarts • Total time: 2½ hours / Active: 1½ hours

I love whipping up soups in the kitchen. This dish is about 10 years old and was conceived out of my need for recipes for my fall pumpkin cooking class. It's always preferable to use fresh pumpkin, but this recipe works with purée from a can as well. To keep this vegetarian, omit the chicken bouillon and substitute vegetable stock for the water.

CINNAMON CREMA

¾	cup	heavy whipping cream
½	teaspoon	ground cinnamon
¼	teaspoon	pure vanilla extract
¼	teaspoon	orange zest

ROASTED PUMPKIN SEEDS

½ to ¾	cup	pumpkin seeds (approximate yield from a 3- to 4-pound pumpkin)
2	tablespoons	water
¼	cup	granulated sugar
½	teaspoon	chili powder
⅛	teaspoon	cayenne
2	teaspoons	ground cinnamon
1	teaspoon	ground nutmeg

PUMPKIN BISQUE

3 to 4	pounds	pumpkin (1 to 1½ pounds pumpkin flesh or 16-ounce can pumpkin purée)
		vegetable oil (for coating)
		salt and pepper to taste
1		carrot, large dice
1	stalk	celery, large dice
½		medium yellow onion
1	teaspoon	ground cinnamon
½	teaspoon	ground cumin
¼	teaspoon	ground allspice
6	cups	water
¼	cup	heavy whipping cream (optional)
1	cube	chicken bouillon
1	teaspoon	fresh sage, finely chopped
½	teaspoon	fresh thyme, chopped
		salt and pepper to taste

1. Make the cinnamon crema. In a heavy sauce pan on medium heat, combine cream, cinnamon, vanilla, and orange zest. Heat to boiling, then simmer over low heat for about 10 minutes. Chill and reserve for service.

2. Make the roasted pumpkin seeds. Preheat the oven to 400°F. Cut the top off the pumpkin, and remove the pulp and seeds. Clean the pumpkin seeds from the pulp, discard pulp and save pumpkin for making the bisque. Spread the seeds out on a baking sheet and roast for about 5 minutes. Stir the seeds and roast again until light golden brown, about another 5 minutes. Remove from the oven, let cool.

CONTINUED >

3. In a small sauce pot over medium-low heat, combine water, sugar, chili powder, cayenne, cinnamon, and nutmeg, and stir until blended. Bring the liquid to a boil and let simmer about 3 to 4 minutes. Remove from the heat, add seeds, and stir until the seeds are coated thoroughly. Spread the seeds over a baking sheet and let cool. After the seeds have cooled and are dry, place them in a food processor and chop to a small, but rough texture. Use this to sprinkle as a garnish.

4. Make the bisque. Raise oven heat to 450°F. Slice the reserved pumpkin into several sections, lightly oil all sides of the pumpkin flesh, and season with salt and pepper. Place the sections on a baking sheet and roast for about 1 hour, until the flesh is tender. Let cool and set aside.

5. Spread the carrot, celery, and onion on a lightly oiled baking sheet and roast until lightly browned, about 35 minutes.

6. Combine the roasted pumpkin (or use the canned purée), roasted vegetables, and dried spices in a stockpot, add water (and heavy whipping cream if desired) and bouillon. Bring the mixture to a boil and simmer for about 30 minutes. Add the fresh herbs.

7. Ladle the mixture into a blender and purée until smooth and silky. Strain the purée for any impurities, and adjust the seasonings to taste.

8. Garnish each serving with cinnamon crema and a pinch of spiced seeds.

Sage Mountain Farm

It wasn't exactly easy to find my friends at Sage Mountain Farm — they're way off in the mountains, in an area called Aguanga, which is about 20 miles east of the city of Temecula. In fact, about two-thirds of the way out there, my GPS just gave up and sent me down a dirt road that wound up leading nowhere!

Being somewhat "off the grid" is just fine for Phil and Juany Noble, who own and operate Sage Mountain. They came out to this remote and very beautiful location to "do their own thing" and, as Phil said, to "enjoy farming in the wilderness — away from all the conventional-type farms."

Back in 2000, the Nobles were struck with what they refer to as "country fever." They moved out of the city and purchased 5 acres in Aguanga. (Evidently, the initial move wasn't all about farming — Phil and Juany also wanted a place where their son Justin could practice his motocross racing.)

The Nobles were dedicated to the idea of organic farming right from the start, and they also wanted to practice and maintain a sustainable lifestyle. They began farming various kinds of vegetables — experimenting with varieties and growing conditions to see what did best in the many microclimates that can make farming a challenge here. During my visit, I saw different kinds of lettuces, herbs, and greens being grown both inside and outside of greenhouses. Phil also showed me his "greenhouse potatoes" and explained how he likes to experiment with new ways of growing things in different environments. "A lot of it is trial and error out here," Phil said. Well, whatever he's doing, it seems to work. Sage Mountain Farm has grown to more than 20 acres on the home farm (all certified organic) and has expanded to include 3 other properties at different elevations. Phil also has a new cattle operation called Sage Mountain Pastures.

In addition to fruits and vegetables, Phil also follows pure organic guidelines to raise steers, chickens, pigs, and goats. Everything at Sage Mountain Farm is watered with the property's own sparkling clean natural well water.

Sage Mountain has made a real name for itself at local Farmers' Markets and through its CSA program, which has more than 200 members. They also supply Whole Foods and other healthy-food stores with their top-quality produce and deliver regularly to a number of restaurants and resorts in the area. Consumers have come to especially love Sage Mountain's heirloom tomatoes, Sage Candy onions, and the special varieties of garlic they produce (especially their hardneck garlic, which I tasted there — it's awesome!).

More information about Sage Mountain Farm is in Featured Organic Farms on page 202.

Left to right: Beautiful radicchio; Phil explains his hothouse potato experiment; rows of incredible spinach; happy chickens.

BUTTERNUT SQUASH GNOCCHI

Serves 6 • Total time: 1½ hours / Active: 1 hour

Way back when, we were buying all of our pasta from outside sources. One day, one of my former sous chefs – Benito Gutierrez – decided to begin making pasta and gnocchi. He started off doing basil gnocchi in the spring and then followed that with this delicious squash variation for the fall.

2	pounds	butternut squash (approximately 1 large)
2	tablespoons	canola or vegetable oil
1		large whole egg
1		large egg yolk
1	cup	all-purpose flour
½	cup	fresh sage, chopped
1	tablespoon	kosher salt
1	teaspoon	freshly ground black pepper
1	cup	freshly grated asiago cheese (or parmesan, gruyère, or similar hard cheese)
2	tablespoons	brown sugar (light or dark)
1½	cups	semolina flour (for rolling)
½	cup	unsalted butter
½	cup	vegetable stock *(See Jeff's Kitchen Advice, Page 19)*

1. Preheat oven to 400°F.

2. Cut the squash in half lengthwise and scoop out the seeds. Spread the 2 tablespoons of oil over a baking sheet and place the squash on it skin side up. Roast in the oven for about 35 minutes, or until the squash is soft. When the squash is cool enough, scoop out the flesh, and process in a food processor until smooth. Place the purée into a clean bowl.

3. In a small bowl, scramble the egg and extra egg yolk, and then mix into the squash. Add ¾ cup of the flour, half of the sage, salt, pepper, ¾ cup of the asiago, and the brown sugar. Mix well and knead with your hands. I've found that a metal spatula or large pastry scraper are great utensils to use to incorporate the flour and eggs into the squash. Scrape underneath and fold until the mixture is a light crumble. Be sure to knead the dough with a gentle touch. If the dough is too tacky, you can add more flour (a sprinkle at a time). I usually end up using the remaining flour, but it all depends on the wetness of the squash, the flour, the time of year, the weather, and whether the gnocchi gods are smiling on you. The dough should be moist but not sticky.

4. On a clean work surface, sprinkle the semolina flour and cut the dough into 8 pieces. With your hands, gently roll each piece into a log roughly the thickness of your thumb. Use a knife to cut pieces every ¾ inch. Dust with a bit more flour. If you want a traditional shape and texture, hold a fork in one hand and place a gnocchi pillow against the tines of the fork, cut ends out. Use your thumb and press in and down on the length of the fork to give them some ridges. Set each gnocchi aside (dust with a bit more flour, if needed).

5. At this point, I recommend that you freeze the gnocchi on a lightly floured baking sheet for 10 to 20 minutes. Make sure the gnocchi aren't touching one another or they'll freeze together.

6. Bring a large pot of water to a boil. Cook the gnocchi in batches by dropping them into the boiling water, roughly 20 at a time. They will let you know when they are cooked because they will pop back up to the top. Fish them out of the water a few at a time with a slotted spoon 10 seconds or so after they've surfaced.

7. In a large sauté pan on medium-high heat, brown the butter. Add the remaining sage and the cooked gnocchi. Season with salt and pepper and add the vegetable stock. Bring the sauce to a boil and add the remaining cheese. Place onto a large serving platter and serve. You can always put some extra cheese on the side.

To Drink with Your Meal...

Wine: The squash, cheese, and butter make this a rich, sweet dish that could pair well with a variety of reds or whites. A **Chardonnay** or **Sauvignon Blanc** with some oak and good acidity levels would work well, as would a lighter-style, fruit-forward red such as a **Sangiovese** or a **Malbec**.
- Robert Mondavi Fumé Blanc
- Hart Sangiovese

Beer: Complement the sweetness of the butternut squash and peppery spice with a robust **Rye Ale**.
- The Bruery's Rugbrod
- Bear Republic's Hop Rod Rye

PUMPKIN RAVIOLI WITH ROASTED CORN CREAM

Serves 6 • Total time: 1½ hours / Active: 45 minutes

This recipe was developed by Terra's first chef, Neil Stuart. After a while, I took it off the menu and replaced it with more seasonal ravioli for springtime, but there was nearly a revolt from my customers. So I put it back on the menu and it's been on ever since. It will never come off.

ROASTED CORN CREAM

2	ears	corn on the cob
2	pints	heavy whipping cream
		salt and pepper to taste

RAVIOLI

4	tablespoons	unsalted butter
⅓	cup	red bell peppers, small dice
⅓	cup	green onions, sliced thin
⅓	cup	leeks, small dice
2½	tablespoons	fennel, small dice
1	tablespoon	fresh garlic, minced
1	tablespoon	ground cumin
1½	tablespoons	chili powder
1	teaspoon	ground cinnamon
1	teaspoon	ground allspice
1	30-ounce can	pumpkin purée
1	teaspoon	kosher salt
¼	teaspoon	freshly ground black pepper
2½	tablespoons	honey
1	package	round gyoza/potsticker wrappers *
1		egg, lightly beaten with a little water (for egg wash)
½	cup	hazelnuts, toasted and chopped
1	tablespoon	canola oil

1. Preheat oven to 375°F. Shuck the corn and place it on a baking sheet in the oven for about 30 minutes, or until slightly caramelized. Cut the corn off the cob and reserve the kernels. Place the cream and corn cobs in a medium sauce pot and bring to a simmer for about 10 minutes. Remove the cobs from the cream, place half of the reserved corn into half the cream and purée the mixture in a blender. Season with salt and pepper and mix with the other half of the cream and the remaining whole kernels. Reserve for service.

2. Make the ravioli. In a large pan over medium heat, melt the butter and sauté the vegetables and garlic until soft. Add the spices and continue sautéing for about 1 minute, stirring constantly so the spices don't burn. Add pumpkin, season with salt and pepper, and heat through. Stir in honey. Transfer to a bowl and reserve.

3. Lay out 8 wonton skins on a clean work surface and brush each one with egg wash. Place about 1 tablespoon of the pumpkin mix in the middle of the wontons. Cover with additional wontons, brush edges with egg wash then press to seal. Finish the remaining ravioli. They can be frozen at this point, if kept tightly sealed, for about 1 month.

4. When ready to cook ravioli, heat the canola oil in a large sauté pan on medium-high heat. Add about 4 ravioli at a time and sauté on the first side for about a minute until a little crispy. Flip the ravioli and sauté for another 30 seconds and then add a little water to create some steam. Place the ravioli on a plate or in a bowl, top with 2 tablespoons of the sauce and about 2 teaspoons of the hazelnuts.

To Drink with Your Meal...

Wine: This is a rich, hearty dish with notes of sweetness and spiciness together. A full-bodied **Chardonnay** with medium oakiness would pair nicely, as would a light to medium-bodied red with good fruit and acid, such as a **Sangiovese** or a **Tempranillo**.
• Clos du Bois Chardonnay
• South Coast Wild Horse II Temporale

Beer: Use the complexity of spices to your advantage and choose a spicy Belgian **Strong Ale**.
• Gouden Carolous
• Allagash Grand Cru

PORK BELLY WITH FAVA BEAN RAGOUT

Serves 4 • Total time: 2½ hours / Active: 45 minutes

This is the top seller from my Kosher catering company — blessed by a rabbi from Israel. Just kidding. Actually, it was developed especially for this book — I did it once or twice as a special, and people loved it. It's one of those dishes that has great flavor but is simple to execute. The fat gives it intensity and juiciness without making the dish heavy — and the meat melts in your mouth.

PORK BELLY

3½	pounds	pork belly
1		medium yellow onion, cut into quarters
1		medium carrot, cut into 2-inch dice
12	cloves	fresh garlic
3	sprigs	mixed fresh herbs
1	tablespoon	star anise
1	stick	cinnamon
4	cups	fresh apple juice
2	cups	fresh orange juice
¼	cup	honey
		salt and pepper to taste

FAVA BEAN RAGOUT

1	cup	peeled carrots, ½-inch dice
1	tablespoon	olive oil
1	cup	medium yellow onion, ½-inch dice
1¼	cups	fresh fava beans, shelled
5	cloves	fresh garlic, roasted
1	teaspoon	ground cumin
1	teaspoon	fresh rosemary, chopped
1	cup	water
½	cup	unsalted butter
		salt and pepper to taste

1. Preheat oven to 375°F.

2. Season with salt and pepper and sear both sides of the pork (fat side first) in a smoking hot sauté pan (about 3 minutes for each side). Remove from the pan.

3. Sauté the vegetables and garlic for 2 minutes before adding the remaining ingredients. Place the pork belly in a baking dish and top with the vegetable and juice mix. Cover with foil and bake for about 2 hours.

4. Remove the pork from the baking dish, strain the liquid, and reduce it on medium heat to make the sauce. *(Hint: it's much easier to braise the pork a day in advance, cool it, and then portion it while cold.)* Cut pork into portions. Each portion should be about a 4- x 4-inch square. To reheat pork you've braised the day before, lightly oil a baking sheet or baking dish and place pork in a 375°F oven for about 20 minutes, or until it's tender yet crispy on the top.

5. Make the ragout. In a large sauté pan on medium heat, sauté the carrots in the olive oil for about 1 minute. *(Hint: always put the harder vegetables in first, especially carrots.)* Add the onion and fava beans and sauté for another minute. Add the remaining ingredients, and bring to a low boil. When sauce begins to thicken after about an hour, skim with a ladle, season with salt and pepper, and you're ready to serve.

6. To plate: Place a half cup of ragout in the middle of a plate. Put a portion of the pork on top, and finish with about 2 tablespoons of sauce per plate.

To Drink with Your Meal…

Wine: The sweetness and fattiness of the pork make it a great companion for a medium-bodied red with good acidity, such as a **Cabernet Franc** or a **Pinot Noir**.
- Saintsbury Pinot Noir
- Fallbrook 33° North Cabernet Franc

Beer: Choose a spicy full-bodied beer that will cut the fatty pork and mirror the complex bouquet of spices. Try a Belgian **Dubbel** or **Strong Dark Ale**.
- Corsendonk Christmas Ale
- Allagash Dubbel

To Drink with Your Meal...

Wine: There are many different sweet and spicy notes going on in this dish, which will often pair best with white wines. The recipe is fairly hearty, so a full-bodied white with some oakiness would stand up well. Try a **Chardonnay** or a **Viognier** — both of which should have some vanilla and floral notes to accent the caramel and cinnamon flavors.
- Au Bon Climat Chardonnay
- Orfila Estate Viognier "Lotus"

Beer: Play up the cinnamon and coriander with a traditional German **Weizenbock**.
- Aventius Weizenbock
- AleSmith 2009 Decadence

CINNAMON-SPICED CHICKEN WITH ROASTED KABOCHA SQUASH

Serves 6 • Total time: 1½ hours / Active: 40 minutes

I developed this dish fairly recently as a new element on the fall menu. Cinnamon and squash are nice fall accents, and the Kabocha (or Japanese pumpkin) has a wonderfully thin skin that roasts nicely and is edible. I add the balsamic caramel and macadamia picada just to give the dish a boost over the top.

ROASTED SQUASH

2		kabocha squash (or any other squash that is available)
¼	cup	olive oil
1	teaspoon	kosher salt
½	teaspoon	freshly ground black pepper

CINNAMON SPICE MIXTURE

2	tablespoons	ground cinnamon
1	tablespoon	ground cumin
1	cup	brown sugar
1	teaspoon	kosher salt
½	teaspoon	black pepper
1	teaspoon	ground ginger
1	tablespoon	chili powder
1½	teaspoons	coriander seed, toasted and ground in a spice grinder

BALSAMIC CARAMEL

1	cup	granulated sugar
¼	cup	water
⅓	cup	balsamic vinegar
⅓	cup	heavy whipping cream
1½	tablespoons	unsalted butter

CHICKEN

6	8-ounce	bone-in, skin-on chicken breasts

MACADAMIA PICADA

1½	cups	macadamia nuts, roasted
1	cup	panko bread crumbs
1	bunch	fresh parsley
		salt and pepper to taste

1. Preheat oven to 425°F.

2. Cut the squash into ½-inch cubes and place them in a medium bowl. Toss with the olive oil, salt, and pepper, and spread onto a baking sheet. Roast for about 20 minutes, or until tender and slightly caramelized.

3. While the squash is roasting, assemble the spice mixture. In a bowl, combine all the cinnamon spice ingredients thoroughly.

CONTINUED >

4. Make the balsamic caramel. In a small sauce pot on medium-high heat, combine the sugar and water and bring to a boil. Reduce heat to low and simmer the mixture for about 5 minutes, until you begin to see a light brown color. At this point, keep a close watch, because the sugar can burn quickly. Allow the mixture to turn brown and just begin to smoke (a matter of seconds) and then slowly add the balsamic. Be careful: you're adding cool liquid to boiling sugar, so it will boil up. Let the mixture melt together, then add the cream. Bring back to a boil and take off the heat. Whisk in the butter and let cool down to warm.

5. Lower oven to 375°F. Coat the chicken liberally with the cinnamon spice mixture on both sides. In a hot sauté pan, sear chicken on each side for about 1 minute. Transfer to a baking dish, place in the oven, and bake for about 30 minutes or until the internal temperature is 150°F to be cooked through.

6. While the chicken is cooking, prepare the macadamia picada. Combine the nuts and parsley in a food processor and chop to a fine consistency. Turn the mixture out into a bowl, add the bread crumbs, and season with salt and pepper.

7. To plate: Put ⅙ of the squash mixture in the center of each plate, and top with a chicken breast. Drizzle balsamic caramel over both the plate and the chicken, and sprinkle the picada on top. Ooh la la!

Butternut squash at Crows Pass Farm in Temecula.

Chef Leah Dibernardo teaches Ty Albright (left), Austin Sigel, and me about the importance of healthy soil.
Students hold fresh herbs from the garden.

Hillcrest Academy

The school garden at Hillcrest Academy is not huge, but it's a part of something very big. This garden – along with 23 others – is supervised and operated in conjunction with Slow Food Temecula, a nonprofit organization that supports 24 school gardens in the Southern California city.

Slow Food is also dedicated to raising awareness and support for local farms, food heritage, and the environment. Slow Food's board consists of parents, farmers, chefs, and health and educational professionals.

Local chef Leah Dibernardo – along with her Slow Food colleagues Rose Watson, Abbey Renke, and Nicolina Alves – volunteers for 20-plus hours each week to visit Temecula schools, supervise learning and teaching activities, and help them care for their gardens. Leah is passionate about what she does: "We do it because we see what poor food does to the body, mind, and spirit of children!" she explains. "Teens are having heart attacks while playing school sports; attention deficit disorder is at an all-time high; and the dramatic increase in children developing type-2 diabetes, due to being overweight, is alarming."

The five raised beds that make up the Hillcrest Academy garden provide kids a firsthand opportunity to learn how to grow food as well as a chance to teach others. The older students regularly take part in teaching the younger ones the ropes. No matter what their ages, all the students agree that what they learn is precious and vital. Gabrielle, 7 years old, says, "I want to be president when I grow up, because somebody has got to do something about bad food ... OMG." Avelaka Macarro, an 8th grader, shares Gabrielle's concerns. "Eating better, eating local, homegrown foods, is simply better for everyone and the environment. I love what Slow Food stands for, and I love doing this work!"

Hillcrest Academy and Temecula's Van Avery Prep both have Slow Food chapters on campus – they are the first schools in the nation to achieve such a goal. Students there are food advocacy leaders, and upon leaving the 8th grade, they will bring stellar garden programs to high schools throughout the area. And that's exactly how it's supposed to work. Plant the seeds. Take some care. And watch it all grow.

STEAK WITH HEIRLOOM BEAN SUCCOTASH AND SMOKED ONION MARMALADE

Serves 4 • Total time: 24+ hours (3 hours cooking) / Active: 90 minutes

I've been using heirloom bean succotash for many years — I use it with pork, leg of lamb, lamb shank, almost anything. It's a different kind of side that works with a wide variety of meats. This is my favorite dish on our menu, because it has so many layers of flavor. The chimichurri sauce has a little spice and tartness; the smoked onion marmalade has a great earthy, sweet flavor; and the beans also have earthiness and nuttiness.

HEIRLOOM BEAN SUCCOTASH

1	cup	dried heirloom beans* (Some I use: appaloosa, scarlet runner, adzuki, anasazi)
3	cups	water
1 to 2	tablespoons	vegetable oil
2	tablespoons	unsalted butter
1		large shallot, minced
2	ears	white corn, cut off the cob
¼	cup	veal demi-glace* *(See Jeff's Kitchen Advice, Page 19)*
		salt and pepper to taste

SMOKED ONION MARMALADE

2		medium yellow onions
¼	cup	white wine vinegar
¼	cup	granulated sugar
1	tablespoon	fresh thyme
1	teaspoon	kosher salt
1	teaspoon	freshly ground black pepper

CHIMICHURRI

½	cup	white wine vinegar
1	cup	olive oil
8	cloves	fresh garlic
2		green chiles, roasted *(See Chef's Tip, Page 27)*
1	teaspoon	red chile flakes (add more if desired)
3	bunches	parsley

MUSTARD GREENS

1	bunch	mustard greens (or any leafy greens), cleaned
1 to 2	tablespoons	olive oil

STEAK

2	pounds	hanger steak

1. Soak the beans for 24 hours. Drain the beans and put them in a large pot or Dutch oven and cover with fresh water — to about 1 inch above the beans. Add the 1 to 2 tablespoons of oil (to prevent foaming and boiling over). Boil gently with the lid tilted until tender, about 1½ to 2 hours. Add hot water as needed to keep the beans just covered with liquid. The best rule is to test frequently during cooking, then decide on your own when beans are tender and taste "done." Keep in mind that when dried beans boil, a foam forms on top of the cooking liquid. This foam is water-soluble protein released from the beans and it will be re-absorbed into the bean cooking liquid. It is not necessary to remove the foam.

CONTINUED >

Wine: Grilled steak and onions are often a great match for Bordeaux-style wines, such as a **Cabernet Sauvignon**, **Merlot,** or **Cabernet Franc**. Depending on how spicy your chimichurri winds up, you may want to stick with lighter, fruitier styles — the spicier, the lighter.

- Franciscan Merlot
- Milagro Cabernet Sauvignon

Beer: Offset the heat from the chimichurri and further develop the flavors of the dish with a full-bodied American **Barleywine**.

- Deschutes Mirror Mirror
- Avery Hog Heaven

2. Make the smoked onion marmalade. Cut each onion into 3 equal slices. If you have a smoker, follow your smoker's instructions for use and smoke the onion slices for approximately 1 ½ to 2 hours at about 200°F. *(If you don't have a smoker, you can sauté the onions on medium heat and add 1 teaspoon of liquid smoke.*)*

3. Chop the onions and put them into a small sauce pot with the salt, pepper, vinegar, and sugar. Cook on medium-high heat for approximately 25 minutes, then lower heat to medium low for an additional 4 minutes.(Make sure to stir often at this point so the onions don't stick and burn). Let the mixture cool to room temperature before adding the freshly chopped thyme. Reserve for plating.

4. In a large sauté pan on medium heat, melt the butter and sweat the shallot for about 1 minute. Add corn, beans, water, and demi-glace. Season with salt and pepper.

5. Make the chimichurri. Put all the ingredients — except the oil — in a blender. Purée until smooth, then slowly add the olive oil until it is combined thoroughly. Makes 1 quart. Sauce will keep in a refrigerator for about 1 week.

6. Sauté mustard greens in olive oil. Season with salt and pepper to taste.

7. Grill the steak to your desired doneness and let it rest, covered, for about 2 to 3 minutes. Slice the meat against the grain and lay it across a half cup of the beans and some of the greens. Top with the marmalade and about 1 tablespoon of chimichurri.

In a field of garlic at Sage Mountain Farm in Aguanga.

Left to right: Agustin Lozano, the garden coordinator, shows me a patch of thriving herbs; Patricia Esteves (left) and Esmeralda Lam (right) demonstrate their potting technique.

Central Elementary School

The garden at Central Elementary in City Heights, named "From the Ground Up," is a natural oasis in a big-city setting. The garden sits in the middle of asphalt and concrete, surrounded by busy city streets and a major freeway. The space was the inspiration of Principal Staci Monreal, who envisioned a school for children that was surrounded by flowers, plants, and trees.

From the Ground Up has been funded in large part by the generous support of the Rice Family Foundation. Under the supervision of Agustin Lozano, the garden coordinator — and a group of children in the school Garden Club — 18 raised beds produce a wide variety of fruits, vegetables, succulents, and flowers. Tomatoes, basil, oregano, thyme, lettuces, snap peas, radishes, and carrots are just some of the bounty — along with beets, onions, bananas, apples, peaches, and many varieties of succulents and flowers.

Every day at lunchtime, the Garden Club skips out to the garden ready to work in the soil. One student said, "We can't wait for Garden Club because it's our chance to make our school even more beautiful. Come see the peas. I bet they are ready to pick today. I'm planting my own at home now that I know how."

Since its inception in 2003, the garden has expanded under the leadership of Principal Cindy Marten, who believes "the garden helps our children learn about gratitude and abundance, as they learn to grow and harvest their own plants to make the school more beautiful. They are using their skills and becoming active, contributing members of a community, which is the ultimate goal of a high-quality education."

I partnered with the Garden Club to do a first-ever "seed to table" program. Cindy and I worked with Gary Petil, director of food services from San Diego Unified School District, to help the Garden Club harvest lettuces, carrots, radishes, and herbs and then to prepare a spring salad mix that was served to 900 children in the school lunch salad bar. Cindy recalls, "When our students realized that the salad on the school salad bar was grown right here in our garden by our own students, every child filled their tray with healthy, homegrown salad greens. There's no better way to promote healthy choices that help our children grow strong minds and healthy bodies."

HERB-ROASTED CHICKEN WITH MUSHROOM RISOTTO AND SPICED PUMPKIN PURÉE

Serves 6 • Total time: 24 to 48 hours / Active: 2 hours

This has been on and off the fall menu for years — it's one of those "comfort food" customer favorites. For the mushroom stock, you can make your own using portobello gills and stems, shiitake stems, or button mushrooms. You can do the risotto the traditional way (adding a little stock at a time), or to save time you can simply pour the stock in all at once.

HERB MARINADE

4	cloves	large fresh garlic, chopped
¼	cup	Worcestershire sauce
2	cups	fresh lime juice
1	cup	fresh sage, chopped
1	cup	fresh mint, chopped
4	cups	olive oil
		salt and pepper to taste

CHICKEN

3		whole roaster chickens, quartered

MUSHROOM RISOTTO

4	cups	mushroom stock (low-sodium, organic, or home-made)
¼	cup	olive oil
2	cups	Arborio rice
2	cups	mixed sliced mushrooms (I use porcini, shiitake, portobello, chanterelle)
2	tablespoons	shallot, chopped
2	tablespoons	fresh garlic, chopped
¼	cup	white wine
		salt and pepper to taste
½	cup	freshly grated asiago cheese

SPICED PUMPKIN PURÉE

1	tablespoon	shallot, minced
1	tablespoon	fresh garlic, minced
1	tablespoon	fresh ginger, grated
¼	teaspoon	ground allspice
¼	teaspoon	ground cinnamon
1	tablespoon	fresh sage, finely chopped
1	tablespoon	fresh thyme, finely chopped
3	cups	chicken or vegetable stock
1		medium tomato, sliced
½	cup	canned pumpkin
2	tablespoons	brown sugar
		salt and pepper to taste
		canola oil (for sautéing)

CONTINUED >

Wine: Roasted chicken with mushrooms and risotto means hearty, earthy flavors that will work nicely with a range of reds that go from light-bodied **(Tempranillo)** to full-bodied **(Cabernet Sauvignon)** or even a fuller-bodied **Syrah**.

- Tablas Creek Syrah
- South Coast Wild Horse Peak Cabernet Sauvignon

Beer: Enhance the earthy and peppery flavors of this dish with a woodsy and spicy Belgian **Brown Ale**.

- Karl Strauss Fullsuit Belgian Brown
- Corsendonk Belgian Brown

Here is a basic procedure for breaking down a chicken:

1. Place the chicken on a cutting board breast side down and make sure the tail is away from you. Hold the tail tightly with the thumb and forefinger of one hand.

2. Use a rigid boning knife to make a single, swift movement, cutting alongside the backbone from the bird's tail to head.

3. Lay the bird flat on the cutting board, and remove the backbone by cutting through the ribs that connect it to the breast.

4. Bend the bird back, breaking the breast bone free.

5. Run your fingers along the bone to separate the breast meat from the bone: pull the bone completely free. Be sure to remove the flexible cartilage completely.

6. Cut through the skin to separate the bird into two halves. At this point, find the junction between the leg and breast on each half and cut through the skin to get the bird into quarters.

7. Cut the tips off the wings and — if you like — cut the thigh and leg into separate pieces by cutting at the joint on each half.

1. Make herb marinade. In a blender, combine the first 5 ingredients. Add the oil in a slow stream and season with salt and pepper. Set aside.

2. Place the chicken in the marinade and be sure to toss and coat all pieces thoroughly. Marinate for at least 24 hours, but not more than 48 hours.

3. Preheat oven to 375°F.

4. Remove the chicken from the marinade and place the pieces on a baking sheet. Season both sides with salt and pepper and roast for 45 minutes, or until an instant-read thermometer reads 155°F.

5. Make the mushroom risotto. In a medium sauce pot on high heat, heat the stock to boiling. In a separate sauce pot, heat the oil on medium heat and sauté the rice for about 3 minutes. Add mushrooms and sauté for 2 minutes. Add shallots and garlic, and sauté for another 3 minutes. Stir constantly to avoid burning. Add the wine to the rice and "burn off" the alcohol by cooking for about 2 minutes. Add all of the heated stock, turn down the heat to medium low, and season with salt and pepper. Simmer and stir until almost all the liquid is gone. Stir in cheese and reserve for service.

6. Make the pumpkin purée. In a medium sauce pot on medium heat, sauté the shallot, garlic, and ginger for about 2 minutes. Add the dried spices and mix well. Add stock and bring to a simmer. Add the rest of the ingredients and return to a simmer for about 20 minutes. In a blender (or with an immersion, or wand, blender) purée the pumpkin mixture, strain it, and reserve.

7. To plate: Pool some pumpkin purée in the center of the plate and spoon some risotto on top. Place chicken on the risotto and serve.

Kabocha squash at Crows Pass Farm in Temecula.

South Coast Winery

As soon as you pull onto the gorgeous grounds of South Coast Winery, you realize this is a place that has everything. In addition to a state-of-the-art winery and a wonderful tasting room, there are also luxurious guest villas, a world-class spa, and a highly acclaimed restaurant. Set in the middle of nearly 30 acres of grapevines, the property welcomes visitors and guests with lush landscaping and dramatic views of the nearby mountains.

In 1981, when Jim Carter first bought a large parcel of land in Temecula, he didn't know exactly what he wanted to do with it. It wasn't until the mid-1990s that he was finally convinced the location would be perfect for growing grapes and making wine.

South Coast began producing wines of notable quality, and Jim decided to expand his program significantly. In 2003, he asked renowned winemaker Jon McPherson to join the team. Today, Jim credits Jon (and winemaker Javier Flores) for the fact that South Coast has achieved outstanding success and received many awards. Jon, in turn, gives Jim Carter a lot of the credit. "The grape quality is always there," Jon says, "and Jim has always supported whatever we needed to get the best grapes possible." Of course, when pressed, Jon admits that the skills and style of the winemaker are important, too. "My approach is very European in style," he explains. "I don't want massive oak or massive alcohol, and I use a mix of oaks for our barrel aging."

Today, the total number of acres under South Coast cultivation has grown to nearly 400. With all those vines, comes an opportunity to grow a stunning variety of grapes and to make wines of every conceivable style. It also allows the winemakers to try some more unique styles, including their wonderful sparkling Gewürztraminer, a sparkling Syrah, and a port made from Muscat. Of course, Jon and Javier also produce a whole host of the best-known varietals, including Sauvignon Blanc, Roussanne, Riesling, Chardonnay, Viognier, Cabernet Sauvignon, Merlot, Syrah, Zinfandel, Grenache, and Tempranillo. "We basically have something to satisfy just about every palate," Jon explains. Like I said: This is a place that has everything.

More information about South Coast Winery is in Featured Wineries on page 203.

Above: The winery is proud of the many awards it has won. Below (left to right): The winery sits in the middle of 30 acres of vines; winemakers Jon McPherson (standing) and Javier Flores; South Coast's wine cellar, filled with wooden casks and stainless steel tanks.

PUMPKIN CRÈME BRÛLÉE

Yields 6 (½-cup) servings • Total time: 3½ hours / Active: 20 minutes

This is a recipe I developed for a cooking class devoted entirely to pumpkin. It's fun because it turns a traditional, classic dessert into a seasonal, holiday treat. At Terra, I've offered this as part of a trio, along with raspberry and espresso crèmes brûlées. Tempering is the key to this recipe: cool the cream a bit, whisk the yolks constantly, and you'll have a nice, creamy crème brûlée.

1¼	cups	heavy whipping cream
1	teaspoon	pure vanilla extract
5		large egg yolks
1	teaspoon	grated nutmeg
6	tablespoons	granulated sugar
½	cup	canned pumpkin purée
¼	cup	raw or brown sugar (for caramelizing)

1. Preheat oven to 350°F. In a medium sauce pan, bring the cream and vanilla to a boil, then take off heat.

2. In a large bowl, whisk together the yolks, nutmeg, and sugar, then add the pumpkin and mix until smooth. When the cream has cooled a bit, add it slowly to the egg mixture, stirring constantly, taking care that the eggs don't lump up and cook.

3. Divide the custard among 6 ramekins and arrange them in a baking dish. Add enough hot water to come halfway up the sides of the ramekins. This is called a water bath. *(See Chef's Tip, Below.)* Bake until the sides of the custards are set but the centers move slightly when shaken (about 45 minutes). Remove from the water bath to cool. Refrigerate at least 2 hours.

4. When ready to serve, preheat the broiler. Sprinkle sugar evenly over custards and broil them about 8 inches from the heat source until the sugar begins to caramelize, but not so much as to burn (about 30 seconds). If you have a kitchen butane torch, you can caramelize each top individually without an oven.

> **Chef's Tip: Water bath.** Water baths are used primarily in baking to help equalize the temperature of what is being baked — usually an egg dish so the eggs don't scramble.

herbs
& lettuces

THE LETTUCE WE SEE TODAY ACTUALLY STARTED OUT AS A WEED around the Mediterranean basin. Served in dishes for more than 4,500 years, lettuce has played a major role in the cuisine of ancient Egypt as well as ancient Greece. (The ancient Greeks believed that lettuce induced sleep, so they served it at the end of the meal, which is what most Europeans do today.) Christopher Columbus is credited with bringing lettuce to the New World.

Today, lettuce is the second-most popular fresh vegetable in the United States behind potatoes. California is known for its innovative salads and microgreens (more than 20 major varieties of lettuce are grown on a large scale in the state), but these aren't recent inventions. In fourteenth-century England, cooks commonly dressed lettuces with oil, vinegar, and salt.

There are 4 main types of lettuce, and within each type there are different varieties:

Butterhead (examples: Boston and Bibb); Crisphead (example: Iceberg); Looseleaf (examples: red leaf and green leaf); and Romaine or Cos.

Herbs are some of the most versatile ingredients available to any chef — their use is limited only by your imagination. The most commonly grown culinary herbs include basil, sage, mint, rosemary, thyme, chive, tarragon, marjoram, dill, parsley, cilantro, and oregano.

These wonderful plants can flavor all kinds of dressings, marinades, soups, and sauces, but can also add unique notes to pastas, breads, or sweet or savory doughs, and can be the basis for many kinds of desserts (basil sorbet is awesome!).

Because they are relatively easy to grow and care for, herbs are probably the most rewarding food plants for even the most novice home gardener. And, for a chef, there are few things more inspiring or satisfying than having fresh-picked herbs to use in a dish.

STRAWBERRY VINAIGRETTE

Yields 3 cups • Total time: 20 minutes / Active: 20 minutes

1	pint	fresh strawberries, trimmed
2	cloves	fresh garlic
¼	cup	fresh mint leaves
¼	cup	fresh basil leaves
1	tablespoon	pickled ginger*
¼	cup	raspberry vinegar
¼	cup	honey
⅛	cup	fresh lime juice
½	cup	canola oil
½	teaspoon	kosher salt
¼	teaspoon	freshly ground black pepper

1. In a blender, purée everything except the oil. In a slow drizzle, add the oil until it is emulsified, then season with salt and pepper. Vinaigrette will keep in the refrigerator for up to 2 weeks.

BEET TRUFFLE VINAIGRETTE

Yields 4 cups • Total time: 65 minutes / Active: 20 minutes

2	pounds	red beets
1½	cups	champagne vinegar
1	cup	water
¾	cup	truffle oil*
⅛	cup	fresh lemon juice
⅛	cup	fresh chives, chopped
		salt and pepper to taste

1. Preheat oven to 450°F. Place the beets in a baking dish with about ¼ cup water, and cover with aluminum foil. Roast them for about 45 minutes, until they are extremely soft and thoroughly cooked. Cool the beets before cutting them into 2- to 3-inch pieces.

2. In a blender, purée the beets with all remaining ingredients — except the chives. Season with salt and pepper. Pour the dressing into a small bowl and add the chives. Reserve for service. Vinaigrette will keep in the refrigerator for up to 2 weeks.

VANILLA BEAN–BLACK PEPPER VINAIGRETTE

Yields 2½ cups • Total time: 24+ hours / Active: 15 minutes

VANILLA OIL

1½	cups	canola or vegetable oil
1		vanilla bean, split and scraped

VINAIGRETTE

¼	cup	black peppercorns, crushed
1	teaspoon	honey
1¼	cups	champagne vinegar
1		vanilla bean, scraped
½	teaspoon	dry mustard
3	tablespoons	granulated sugar
1	tablespoon	kosher salt
2	stalks	fresh lavender flowers and leaves

1. Make the vanilla oil. Heat oil in a small sauce pot until it reaches 110°F. Remove from heat. Add the vanilla bean and let stand at room temperature for at least 24 hours. Remove the vanilla bean.

2. In a blender, purée everything except the oil. In a slow drizzle, add the oil until it is emulsified. Vinaigrette will keep in the refrigerator for up to 2 weeks.

FARMER'S SALAD

Serves 8 • Total time: 20 minutes / Active: 20 minutes

We originally called this the "Market Salad" because we would feature whatever we found fresh and interesting at the local market that day. These days, I like to highlight the amazing produce I get from Suzie's, Crows Pass, Be Wise, and a bunch of the other terrific organic farms that supply us on a regular basis—so now I call it the "Farmer's Salad."

CHAMPAGNE-HERB VINAIGRETTE

1		shallot, minced
¼	cup	fresh mixed herbs, chopped
1	cup	champagne vinegar
¾	tablespoon	tomato paste
½	cup	fresh orange juice
¾	tablespoon	granulated sugar
¾	teaspoon	kosher salt
½	tablespoon	freshly ground black pepper
2	cups	olive oil

SALAD

1	pound	mixed greens (I use escarole, tatsoi, arugula)
½	pound	baby radishes, peeled, blanched, and chopped
½	pound	baby beets, roasted, peeled and quartered
½	pound	English peas
½	pound	Romanesco cauliflower
½	pound	broccoli rabe
½	pound	tangerine slices, peeled, or Meiwa kumquats, sliced
		salt and pepper to taste

1. Make the vinaigrette. In a large bowl, combine everything except the oil. Pouring in a slow stream, gradually whisk in the oil until incorporated. Vinaigrette will keep in the refrigerator for up to 2 weeks.

2. In a large bowl, lightly dress the lettuces and vegetables with the vinaigrette, season with salt and pepper, and serve.

Remember: The amount of vinaigrette needed will vary depending on your choice of lettuce, so make sure to go little by little. You can always add more!

TERRA'S HOUSE SALAD

Serves 8 • Total time: 80 minutes / Active: 20 minutes

This classic rendition of a nut-and-cheese salad has been on the menu for at least 6 years. The combination of sweet dressing, candied nuts, gorgonzola cheese, and peppery arugula makes it a hands-down customer favorite. It's another one of those items that I sell so much of, I could never even think of taking it off the menu.

CANDIED PECANS

1		large egg white
1	tablespoon	water
1	cup	granulated sugar
¾	teaspoon	kosher salt
1	teaspoon	ground cinnamon
1	pound	pecan halves

HONEY-WALNUT-HERB VINAIGRETTE

Yields 2½ cups

¾	cup	honey
¾	cup	apple cider vinegar
1⅛	cups	walnut oil
⅛	cup	shallots, minced
⅛	cup	fresh thyme, chopped
½	teaspoon	kosher salt
¼	teaspoon	freshly ground black pepper

SALAD

1	pound	arugula
½	pound	radicchio, sliced
1½	cups	crumbled gorgonzola cheese
2	cups	candied pecans

1. Preheat oven to 250°F.

2. Grease a baking sheet. In a bowl, whip the egg white and water until frothy. In a separate bowl, mix sugar, salt, and cinnamon. Add pecans to the egg whites, coating them well. Remove the nuts, and toss them in the sugar mixture. Spread the nuts out evenly on the baking sheet. Bake for 1 hour, stirring every 15 minutes. Make sure they don't burn.

3. Make the vinaigrette. In a blender, combine the first 3 ingredients. Pour into a bowl, and mix in the shallots and thyme. Season with salt and pepper. Vinaigrette will keep in the refrigerator for up to 2 weeks.

4. In a large bowl, lightly dress the lettuces with the vinaigrette, season with salt and pepper, top with cheese and pecans, and serve.

To Drink with Your Meal...

Wine: The nuts and cheese in this salad provide hearty components that would pair wonderfully with a crisp but medium-bodied white, such as a **Marsanne** or **Viognier.**
• Hart Roussanne
• Stag's Leap Viognier

Beer: A malty **Lager** will have a bit of sweetness to match the pecans but enough character to stand up to the gorgonzola.
• Ballast Point Calico Lager
• Karl Strauss Amber Lager

Robin gives me the up-close-and-personal tour of Suzie's fields.

Suzie's and Sun Grown Farm

We set out one chilly, drizzly Saturday morning – heading south toward Imperial Beach – to visit Suzie's and Sun Grown, where I get a lot of the produce I use for Terra.

We met up with Robin Taylor, who – with his wife Lucila de Alejandro – owns Sun Grown and Suzie's organic farms. Robin welcomed us with a small clamshell container filled with little acorn-looking things. "Here, try some – just a little bit, though. No one can eat an entire button." Robin explained that they were called Sansho buttons, and they were part of the cress family. I popped a small piece in my mouth – whoa! It was like nothing I had ever tasted. Weird. Spicy, peppery, tangy, and numbing. (You get to try some really cool stuff when you hang out with growers!)

Cool stuff is what Robin is all about – he's the sprouts, grasses, and microgreens expert, and he loves experimenting with all kinds of plants. We got a tour through his hothouses, each filled with flats and flats of seeds – all at one stage of sprouting or another. The different tastes and flavors were amazing. Beet microgreens. Wheat grass. Even greens sprouting from popcorn kernels (really good!).

Before heading to Suzie's, Robin wanted to show off his huge compost piles (plant matter only). When we saw the piles, we knew why he was so proud of them — they were growing all kinds of amazing greens, and they were huge! I had the best compost pile salad I've ever had. (The red and green mustard greens were awesome!)

Suzie's is only a few miles away. When you pull up to the fields, you realize that all this gorgeous produce is growing smack dab in between the huge border fence at the U.S.-Mexico border and the compound of the U.S. Border Patrol. But, what a beautiful buffer zone: broccoli, kale, carrots, radicchio, peas, spring mix lettuces, and rows and rows of gorgeous strawberries — more than 100 varieties of certified organic fruits and vegetables.

I have been using Suzie's wonderful organic produce for years, but this was the first time I had a chance to see where it actually sits in the ground. I have to say, it was really great to make the connection between what I eat and cook in the restaurant and what was sprouting up from the earth in this beautiful spot.

More information about Suzie's and Sun Grown Farm is in Featured Organic Farms on page 202.

Above: Robin pulls some samples off the tastiest compost pile ever. Below (left to right): Delicious popcorn sprouts emerge; checking out Sun Grown's sprout vats; Suzie's gorgeous mustard greens.

Serves 8 • Total time: 1 hour / Active: 1 hour

I first came up with this recipe for a cooking class I was about to teach. I had recently seen another chef use the technique of making a mousse with chicken and herbs, so I was inspired to create something similar. I've included it here because it's relatively easy for the home cook to do, it looks impressive when you cut it, and it also tastes great.

ARUGULA PESTO

4	cups	arugula, chopped
1	cup	fresh sage, chopped
2	cups	pine nuts or walnuts, toasted
1	teaspoon	freshly ground black pepper
½	tablespoon	kosher salt
1½	cups	extra virgin olive oil

CHICKEN

2	cups	fresh basil, chopped
11	6- to 8-ounce	boneless, skinless chicken breasts
8		large egg whites
1½	tablespoons	kosher salt
3	teaspoons	freshly ground black pepper
2	tablespoons	canola oil

1. Put all of the pesto ingredients, except the oil, into a food processor. Purée until smooth, and slowly drizzle oil in while the machine is running. Reserve for service.

2. Preheat oven to 400°F.

3. Put the basil into a food processor and pulse 4 times.

4. Chop 3 chicken breasts into 1-inch pieces. Add the chicken pieces and egg whites to the basil and purée until smooth. Season with 1 teaspoon of salt and ½ teaspoon pepper and set the mousse aside. Cover each of the remaining 8 breasts with plastic wrap and pound each one to a thickness of about ½ inch. Place 1 to 2 tablespoons of mousse on top of each breast, roll up, and wrap with kitchen twine. Season with remaining salt and pepper.

5. In a sauté pan over high heat, sear each chicken roll in the canola oil, then finish them in the oven for about 12 minutes or until the internal temperature reaches 150°F to 155°F. After removing the rolls from the oven, let them rest for about 2 minutes. Evenly slice the chicken and serve with pesto.

CARLSBAD MUSSELS WITH CHARDONNAY-HERB SAUCE

Serves 4 to 6 • Total time: 45 minutes / Active: 45 minutes

Thinking local, I've made a commitment to always buy mussels from Carlsbad Aquafarms — on the coast about 40 minutes north of the restaurant. They also breed clams, seaweed, oysters, and abalone, which they ship all over the country. They supply me with Mediterranean black mussels that are deliciously sweet and tender if you don't overcook them. Two hints for this dish: First, the key is caramelizing the vegetables — all the flavor in this dish comes from that. Second, remember that mussels cook at different times — so watch them carefully, and once they open, take them out and reserve them until the last ones are done. Then put them all back in the broth before serving.

¼	cup	canola oil
1	cup	red bell pepper, sliced
1	cup	red onion, sliced
1	cup	poblano pepper, sliced
4	pounds	Carlsbad mussels, cleaned of the beards
2	tablespoons	fresh garlic, minced
1	tablespoon	fresh thyme, chopped
1	tablespoon	fresh rosemary, chopped
2½	cups	crisp chardonnay (not too oaky)
¼	cup	heavy whipping cream
1	teaspoon	kosher salt
1	teaspoon	freshly ground black pepper

1. Heat the oil in a sauté pan until the oil is smoking. Add the peppers and onions and sauté until they start to lightly brown (it's crucial that the vegetables begin to caramelize and turn brown). Add the mussels, garlic, and herbs, and deglaze with the white wine. Add the cream, cover, and cook for about 2 minutes or until almost opened fully. Taste the sauce, and season with salt and pepper, as needed. Continue cooking until the mussels are completely opened and then serve.

Note: Remember that mussels all cook at different rates — some open first, others need more time. As the mussels open, take them out of the liquid and reserve them until the others are all open. Be sure to discard any that do not open.

To Drink with Your Meal...

Wine: The richness of this creamy dish — in addition to the fact that there is chardonnay in the sauce — makes this recipe an ideal candidate for **Chardonnay** or, for a lighter, crisper alternative, a **Fumé Blanc**.
- Talley Chardonnay
- South Coast Estate Fumé

Beer: Creamy sauces tend to pair well with crisper, dryer beers that can cut through the richness to refresh the palate. Try a **Saison** or **IPA**.
- North Coast Le Merle
- Founders Centennial IPA

MIXED MUSHROOM RAGOUT WITH HERB-POLENTA CAKE

Serves 4 to 6 • Total time: 4 hours / Active: 1½ hours

The idea behind this side dish is simple — simple, earthy flavors that highlight fresh, good-quality mushrooms. Most often, I use oysters, enokis, and creminis for this recipe, but you can easily mix in or substitute almost any kind of mushroom, including shiitakes, portobellos, chicken-of-the woods, lobster mushrooms, or even earthy morels. Use the best wild mushrooms in season, when available, or sustainably grown hydroponic varieties.

HERB-POLENTA CAKES

½	cup	olive oil
2	cups	yellow onions, diced
2	cups	assorted chard, cut into 2-inch pieces
12	cups	chicken stock or vegetable stock
4	cups	polenta or yellow cornmeal
¼	cup	fresh rosemary, chopped
¼	cup	fresh thyme, chopped
¼	cup	fresh basil, chopped
¼	cup	scallions, sliced
1	cup	freshly grated asiago or parmesan cheese
1	tablespoon	kosher salt
½	tablespoon	freshly ground black pepper

MUSHROOM RAGOUT

⅛	cup	extra virgin olive oil or grapeseed oil
1	pound	mixed mushrooms
½	pound	leeks, washed and cut into ½-inch dice
1	teaspoon	kosher salt
½	teaspoon	freshly ground black pepper
¼	cup	white wine (any non-oaky kind that you would drink)
8	tablespoons	unsalted butter

1. In a large pot, sauté the onions and chard in the oil until tender. Add the stock and bring to a boil. Whisk in the cornmeal slowly to avoid lumps. Stir over medium-high heat. Add the remaining ingredients and cook until thick. You can serve this creamy polenta now or continue to make the cakes. Pour the mixture into a plastic-lined baking dish or loaf pan and chill (at least 2 to 3 hours). When ready to serve, cut the polenta into discs or squares and reheat them on a hot griddle or in a sauté pan.

2. For the ragout: in a sauté pan over medium-high heat, add olive oil and stir in the mushrooms and leeks. Continue cooking until tender, about 2 minutes. Season with salt and pepper and add the white wine. Cook for another minute, until the wine burns off slightly. To finish the sauce, whisk in the butter and emulsify. Serve over the hot polenta cakes.

ROSEMARY ROAST DUCK WITH ROASTED CAULIFLOWER PURÉE

Serves 4 to 6 • Total time: 4½ hours / Active: 45 minutes

The duck part of this recipe was created partly by happy accident — many good recipes are! I was doing a cooking class and decided to base the class on "cooking off the shelf" — so I found a bunch of ingredients to make an herb crust, put it together with the duck, and got this! The roasted cauliflower purée was not originally developed to accompany the duck, but so many people asked me to put it in the book, that I had to find a place for it. Lots of people have done their version of cauliflower purée, but — by roasting it first — the dish takes on a whole new dimension.

ROASTED CAULIFLOWER PURÉE

4	heads	cauliflower, cleaned, cut into 3- to 4-inch pieces
½	cup	olive or canola oil
1	teaspoon	kosher salt
½	teaspoon	freshly ground black pepper

ROSEMARY ROAST DUCK

2		whole ducks, cut in half with backbones removed (*See Chef's Tip, Page 110*)
2	teaspoons	kosher salt
2	teaspoons	freshly ground black pepper
¼	cup	fresh rosemary, finely chopped
½	cup	carrot, chopped
½	cup	onion, chopped (any kind is fine)
½	cup	celery, chopped

PARMESAN CRUST

¾	cup	freshly grated parmesan cheese (or other hard cheese)
¼	cup	fresh rosemary, finely chopped
⅓	cup	panko bread crumbs
½	tablespoon	kosher salt
½	teaspoon	freshly ground black pepper

1. Preheat oven to 475°F. In a large bowl, coat cauliflower evenly with oil. Season with salt and pepper. Place the cauliflower on a baking sheet, floret side down, and roast until well-browned and caramelized, approximately 40 minutes. When cool enough to handle, purée the cauliflower in a food processor. If the purée is too thick, drizzle in some additional oil until smooth. Adjust seasoning as needed, and reserve for service.

2. Lower oven to 350°F. Poke the ducks all over with a fork. Season both sides with salt and pepper. Line a baking dish with the rosemary and all of the vegetables. Lay the ducks on top, and bake for about 3 hours, or until the duck is crispy. Twist the leg bone and if it moves easily, it's ready.

3. While the duck is cooking, make the parmesan crust — combine the hard cheese, rosemary, bread crumbs, and salt and pepper. Separate the leg and breast portions of the ducks. Pack the parmesan crust on the outside of the ducks and return them to the oven for 10 minutes or until slightly brown.

4. Serve duck with the roasted cauliflower purée.

To Drink with Your Meal...

Wine: The hearty, rich flavors of this dish are perfectly suited to a medium-bodied red, such as a **Mourvèdre,** a **Zinfandel,** or a **Pinot Noir.**
- Ravenswood Zinfandel Belloni
- Mueller "Emily's Cuvée" Pinot Noir.

Beer: The richness of the duck, combined with the assertive rosemary, demands a crisp lager with an herbal character. Try a Czech **Pilsner** or, even better, an **Imperial Pilsner.**
- Pilsner Urquell
- Karl Strauss Whistler Imperial Pils

Fallbrook Winery

One sunny February afternoon – after spending a wonderful morning at Blue Heron Farm – I traveled over to a nearby winery in Fallbrook. It is, in fact, the only winery in Fallbrook. I had been invited by the owner, Ira Gourvitz, to come out for a personal tour and an *al fresco* lunch on the winery's patio. (Who could turn that down?)

Ira told me that, when he first took over his wine property in Fallbrook, he had a lot of work to do. The place had previously been home to a failing sparkling wine producer, so one of the first orders of business was to replant the vineyards with more promising varietals – notably the classic Bordeaux grapes of Cabernet Sauvignon, Merlot, Cabernet Franc, Petite Verdot, and Malbec.

The next major challenge, as Ira explained, was to convince the world that high-quality wines could actually be produced in this little-known and somewhat isolated region of Southern California. Ira knew that the vineyard's unique location – 800 feet up in the Pala Mesa Mountains and less than 12 miles from the Pacific Ocean – would provide the raw materials he needed to make great wine. Evidently, the topography of the region creates a microclimate that's ideal for growing grapes; the soil is mostly decomposed granite, and the ocean breezes provide consistent and moderate temperatures throughout the growing season, with the warm days and cool nights that most grape varieties love.

While he was waiting for his newly planted vines to mature, Ira began vinifying chardonnay with grapes he had purchased from Monterey's famed Sleepy Hollow Vineyard. (Before coming to Fallbrook, Ira had owned a chardonnay vineyard in Sonoma, so he was no slouch with chardonnay.) Soon, Fallbrook Winery added bottlings of Cabernet Sauvignon, Sauvignon Blanc, and Merlot to their roster. The winemaker, Duncan Williams, is a master at using different grapes to make great blends, and his talents shined through in these wines. It wasn't long before Fallbrook Winery began to win gold medals and other awards at major wine competitions.

In 2009, Fallbrook released its first estate grown wines, which are collectively called 33° North Estate wines. The Bordeaux-style blend is called BDX, named for the markings used to identify the blend while in barrels. Other 33° North wines include estate-grown Cabernet Franc, Malbec, Merlot, Syrah, and Sangiovese Rosé.

Reaction to Fallbrook's debut with estate-grown wines was nothing short of phenomenal. BDX won a gold medal at the 2009 Sommelier International Wine Challenge, where silver medals went to the Cabernet Franc, Malbec, and Merlot. The Sangiovese Rosé took the platinum medal at the 2009 Winemaker's Challenge Competition, where the Fallbrook Reserve Cabernet Sauvignon won gold, and BDX, Syrah, and the Reserve Sauvignon Blanc won silvers. BDX also won silver medals at both the Monterey International Wine Competition and the Grand Harvest Awards. Not bad for their first bottlings!

Today, Ira has the help of a second expert winemaker, Vernon Kindred, who continues to expand the depth and breadth of the wines Fallbrook can offer. (Vernon let me taste their 2009 Sangiovese straight from the barrel — it was awesome!) Vernon and Duncan are constantly tasting, testing, and evaluating possible new blends as well as new varietals. A second vineyard, the Mela Ranch Vineyard, was planted with Sauvignon Blanc and Syrah, and a third estate vineyard — Jazwa — has been planted with Cabernet Sauvignon and Merlot.

Today, Fallbrook Winery is one of the leaders in California's emerging South Coast wine region. The success of their estate wines proves that the area can produce fine wines of the highest quality, and from many different varietals. "It's all very exciting and gratifying," Ira explained over sandwiches and salad on the patio deck. "We've known all along that this region was special, and now we're proving it. This is what it's all about. Everything we've done to this point has been about the 33° North Estate wines."

More information about Fallbrook Winery is in Featured Wineries on page 203.

Co-winemaker Vernon (left) and Ira let me sample a house blend.

root vegetables

TRADITIONALLY, WINTER IS THE SEASON FOR ROOT VEGETABLES. That's partly because root vegetables are at their best when temperatures are cool, sometimes even cold, and many even do well with light to heavy frosts. The seeds of these vegetables also germinate well in cool soils. Root vegetables also rule the winter season because many of them provide the basis for hearty, soul-and-body-warming meals.

There are numerous categories of root vegetables, but we focus on two main groups here: the "true roots" and the "tuberous roots." The true roots include many common cold-weather vegetables, such as carrots, beets, parsnips, turnips, rutabagas, and fennel. Some of the less common — but no less tasty — members of this group include the daikon radish, jicama, and salsify. The generally high sugar content of many true roots makes them perfect for roasting on their own, or adding to dishes as a sweet accompaniment.

The tubers and tuberous root vegetables include winter staples such as potatoes, yams, and sweet potatoes. Also included in this grouping are cassava and Jerusalem artichoke. These starchy vegetables are incredibly versatile; they're commonly baked or roasted on their own, used to create thick soups and stews, or cooked in any number of other ways, including deep-frying, pan-frying, or boiling and mashing.

Unlike many other vegetables (and fruits), root vegetables tend to be hardy and long-lasting. When shopping for root vegetables, choose the ones that are firm — even hard. A soft potato, mushy fennel bulb, or limp carrot is an undesirable sign of age. When you get them home, you can store root vegetables in the fridge or any cool, preferably dark, place for some time. The exact amount of time will vary by vegetable and how fresh it was when you bought it.

Be sure to wash all root vegetables thoroughly — they've spent most of their lives in the dirt! — and scrape or peel off any green sprouts or shoots that may grow out of the crevices in the skin's surface.

COCOA-RUBBED LAMB SHANK WITH ROOT VEGETABLE HASH

Serves 4 • Total time: 4 hours / Active: 45 minutes

I've been doing this one for a long time — more than a decade. The idea came to me as a variation of a mole. Instead of a chocolate paste or sauce, I decided to do a rub (and I added the cinnamon because it pairs so well with chocolate). I use hind shanks for this recipe — they're a little larger, thicker, and meatier than the fore-shanks. The cocoa rub also works well with steaks — but take care when searing or grilling, because the cocoa can burn easily. All of this can be made 1 or 2 days in advance and put together when you're ready to serve.

ROASTED FENNEL

2	bulbs	baby fennel (or 1 large bulb, cut into quarters)
1	tablespoon	olive oil
1	teaspoon	kosher salt
½	teaspoon	freshly ground black pepper

COCOA RUB

1	tablespoon	cocoa powder
1	tablespoon	ground cinnamon
½	tablespoon	chili powder
¼	tablespoon	garlic powder
⅛	tablespoon	kosher salt
⅛	tablespoon	freshly ground black pepper
½	tablespoon	brown sugar

LAMB

4	14-ounce	lamb hind shanks
1	750-milliliter bottle	ruby port wine
¾	cup	fresh rosemary, chopped
¾	cup	fresh thyme, chopped
1		medium carrot, chopped
1		medium celery stalk, chopped
1		large brown onion, chopped
3	cloves	fresh garlic
5		black peppercorns

ROOT VEGETABLE HASH

1½	pounds	mixed root vegetables (parsnips, turnips, celery root, carrots, beets), peeled, cut into ½-inch dice
2	tablespoons	olive oil
1	tablespoon	fresh rosemary
1	tablespoon	fresh thyme
1	teaspoon	fresh garlic, minced
		salt and pepper to taste

CONTINUED >

CARAMELIZED APPLES

¼	cup	unsalted butter
¼	cup	granulated sugar
3		Gala apples, cored and sliced, skin on

1. Preheat oven to 425°F.

2. Cut the tops off the fennel bulbs and cut the bulbs in half. In a bowl, toss with the olive oil, salt, and pepper and place onto a baking sheet. Roast the pieces in the oven for about 25 minutes, or until the fennel is slightly caramelized. Reserve for service.

3. Reduce oven to 375°F.

4. Mix all the rub ingredients together in a bowl. Rub the shanks thoroughly and set aside.

5. Heat a large sauté pan with oil until smoking and sear the lamb shanks on all sides until browned. Remove shanks from pan. Add the carrot to hot sauté pan for 1 minute. Next add celery and onion and continue sautéing for another 3 to 4 minutes until slightly caramelized. Stir in garlic and sauté for another minute. Then place the shanks and vegetables in a large roasting pot with the port wine, rosemary, thyme, and peppercorns. Cover with foil and bake for 3½ hours or until fork tender.

6. Take the lamb out of the pot and strain the liquid into a small sauce pot. On medium-high heat, reduce the liquid to a sauce consistency.

7. Make the vegetable hash. In a large stock pot, boil the root vegetables for approximately 10 minutes, then strain them into an ice bath to stop the cooking. Heat the oil in a large sauté pan on high heat, add the root vegetables and sauté for about 1 minute. Add the herbs, garlic, and season with salt and pepper. Reserve for service.

8. Make the caramelized apples. In a sauté pan on low heat, melt the butter, then add the sugar and apples. Stir until the apples caramelize (it should take about 20 minutes to cook off the liquid and caramelize). Reserve for garnish.

9. To plate: Place about ½ cup of the hash into a bowl. Lay a lamb shank over the hash and prop a piece of fennel on the shank. Ladle about ⅛ cup of the reduced sauce onto the shank and top with some caramelized apple.

Crows Pass Farm

Every evening in the fall, scads of crows roost in the sprawling vineyards of Temecula's wine country. As they travel from one location to the other, the crows pass over the fields where David and Tina Barnes grow their organic fruits and vegetables. Hence, the name.

In 1991, David and Tina began farming a portion of unused land that was part of an 80-acre parcel owned by David's father. As Tina recalls, "The farm began with a fistful of strawberry plants, carrots, peas, and a dependable truck." They learned the ropes like most young farmers do: through trial and error and by becoming a part of Southern California's farming community. They participated in local Farmers' Markets for about 10 years before focusing more and more on chef-direct relationships. Tina says it's very rewarding to work with so many of San Diego's finest chefs. "Our hard work and commitment to quality is truly appreciated by chefs, and they pass that appreciation on through their dishes."

Crows Pass is currently rotating about 15 acres of land, but they plan to get up to about 40 acres in the near future. They produce crops year round, and are known for a number of seasonal specialties, such as their Israeli melons, vintage strawberries, Spanish onions, asparagus, and mulberries. Other favorites include baby carrots, turnips, radishes, mustard greens, and spinach. Small orchards on the property grow apples (including Japanese apples), figs, and various kinds of stone fruit.

As David and Tina look toward the future, they plan to put more acres under cultivation and expand the network of chefs and restaurants they work with. But, their dreams are not only about expansion. They also hope to play a part in educating people about the benefits of organic farming. As Tina put it, "We want to build an educational farm center that teaches the importance of farming and celebrates the joy of good food."

More information about Crows Pass Farm is included in Featured Organic Farms on page 202.

Above: David tells me about the benefits of composting.
Below (left to right): delicata squash, watermelon radish, and young garlic plants.

RATATOUILLE PILLOWS WITH GRUYÈRE AND OVEN-ROASTED TOMATOES

Serves 4 as an appetizer • Total time: 2½ hours / Active: 2 hours

This was created for a cooking class I did way back in 2003, when I wanted to feature foods that were wrapped in different ways. Phyllo dough is one of those items some people are frightened by. I like teaching people about phyllo dough because it's easy to use, it's super versatile, and it adds great texture. This ratatouille is all about simple, fresh vegetables that take on an added flavor dimension when roasted.

RATATOUILLE MIXTURE

¼	cup	fresh basil, chiffonade
1	tablespoon	fresh garlic, minced
¼	cup	olive oil
6		large tomatoes, roasted
¼	cup	baby carrots, blanched and chopped
¼	cup	eggplant, grilled and chopped
¼	cup	zucchini, grilled and chopped
		salt and pepper to taste

PILLOWS

8	tablespoons	unsalted butter
1	package	frozen phyllo dough
¼	cup	freshly grated gruyère cheese

1. Preheat oven to 375°F.

2. In a large sauté pan over medium heat, cook the basil and garlic in the olive oil for 1 to 2 minutes. Add all the vegetables and toss until combined. Season with salt and pepper and chill.

3. Melt the butter. Take a sheet of phyllo dough and cut it into thirds lengthwise. Brush each third with melted butter. Place about 1 tablespoon of the ratatouille mixture at one end of the phyllo strip. Top the filling with a teaspoon of the cheese and roll upward diagonally into a triangle shape, buttering the top as you fold. Continue with remaining phyllo strips, and brush the pillow tops with more butter before baking. Place on a buttered baking sheet and bake until golden brown, about 15 minutes.

To Drink with Your Meal...

Wine: Caramelization from the fennel and sweetness from the butternut squash make this hearty dish a candidate for a range of either whites or reds. For white, the medium-bodied **Viognier** would work nicely — for a red, go with a lighter style **Zinfandel**.

- Orfila Estate Viognier "Lotus"
- Rancho Zabaco Zinfandel

Beer: Choose a beer with good caramel and toasted malt flavors to complement the caramelized fennel and sweetness of the butternut squash. An **Amber Lager** or **Altbier** will both work.

- Anderson Valley Boont Amber
- Coney Island Lager

CARAMELIZED FENNEL AND ROASTED BUTTERNUT SQUASH SALAD

Serves 6 to 8 • Total time: 1½ hour / Active: 45 minutes

This dish was developed for a Thanksgiving menu — and was so popular I actually used it again the next Thanksgiving. Not only is this a beautiful picture, but the flavors of the rice, roasted squash and caramelized fennel make for an awesome fall salad. Remember, there's not a lot of water in fennel, so the trick to caramelizing it is to go low (heat) and slow.

3	cups	water
1	teaspoon	kosher salt
1	cup	uncooked wild rice
2	cups	butternut squash, peeled and cut into ¼- to ½-inch cubes
½	cup	olive oil
6	bulbs	fennel, julienned
1	head	butter lettuce
¼	cup	fresh basil, chiffonade
1	cup	dried cranberries
¼	cup	honey or agave sweetener*
		salt and pepper to taste

1. Preheat oven to 425°F.

2. Bring 3 cups water to a boil in a large pot with the salt and wild rice. Reduce heat to maintain a low boil. Cook the rice until tender, about 30 minutes. Drain in a sieve or fine-mesh colander. (Boiled wild rice tends to have tender, but intact kernels.) Allow the rice to cool.

3. In a medium bowl, toss the squash with ⅛ cup of olive oil, salt, and pepper. Place the coated pieces on a baking sheet and roast in the oven for about 20 minutes or until tender and slightly caramelized.

4. Heat another ⅛ cup of olive oil in a medium sauté pan over medium-high heat. Add the fennel and cook for 2 to 3 minutes while stirring. Turn the heat down to low and continue to cook and stir for another 7 to 8 minutes, or until very soft and slightly caramelized. *(Note: fennel will not caramelize like onions do because it doesn't have as much sugar.)*

5. Take the head of lettuce and pull apart 6 to 8 leaves and keep them intact to act as the cups for the salad. In a large bowl, combine the cooked rice, squash, fennel, basil, cranberries, the remaining olive oil, honey or agave sweetener; season with salt and pepper, toss well, and serve in a lettuce cup or two.

ROASTED BEET AND WATERMELON SOUP

Yields 4 quarts • Total time: 1½ hours / Active: 30 minutes

Watermelon soup is a traditional summer soup, and beet soup is traditionally for fall or winter. One of my sous chefs, back in 1999, had an idea for this summer to fall transition — served cold. The soup has won many fans (one of my most devoted regulars, Karan Greenwald, loves it) and people ask me for the recipe all the time. The garnish adds extra flavor and color, but it's not absolutely necessary.

SOUP

1½	pounds	red beets
1		large golden beet
½	cup	canola oil
1½	pounds	red watermelon, skinned, seeded, and chopped
½	cup	fresh basil, chopped
1		lemon, juiced
1	tablespoon	fennel seed, toasted
⅛	cup	honey
		salt and pepper to taste

GARNISH

¼	cup	mirin (sweet cooking rice wine) *
1	teaspoon	fresh ginger, grated
1		white or yellow peach

1. Preheat oven to 375°F.

2. Toss all the beets in the canola oil, lay them out on a baking sheet or in a baking dish, and roast them for 1 hour or until tender. Beets vary in size — check by piercing them with a toothpick or skewer and, if they come out cleanly, the beets are done. Remove the beets from the oven and cover with plastic wrap. Reserve the large golden beet for the garnish, step 4.

3. Once the beets are cool enough to handle, peel off the skins with a towel. Chop the red beets and purée in batches in a blender with the watermelon (it is necessary to squeeze watermelon into the blender to allow the juice to help purée the beets). Add the basil, lemon, fennel seed, and honey, little by little in each batch. Season with salt and pepper, strain and reserve for service.

4. Make the garnish. Chop the cooled and peeled golden beet into small pieces. Purée the beet, ginger and peach in a blender until smooth and top the soup with a dollop of the purée.

Note: When making cold soups like this, it is always best to let the flavors develop for 24 hours before straining.

To Drink with Your Meal...

Wine: Roasted beets provide a sweet and earthy flavor foundation for this dish. The honey and the lemon components would pair well with a wine that has some "honey" oakiness as well as some citrus — such as a light- to medium-bodied **Chardonnay** or a **Sauvignon Blanc** that has been oaked.
- La Crema Chardonnay
- South Coast Estate Fumé

Beer: While the beets provide an earthy character, focus your beer pairing on the watermelon and citrus elements. Try a Bavarian **Hefeweizen**.
- Mission Hefeweizen
- Paulaner Hefeweizen

SEA BASS TIPI TAPA WITH CARROT PURÉE

Serves 6 • Total time: 2 hours / Active: 1 hour

This has been on our menu since the first day we opened — it's another recipe that was developed by Neil Stuart, our first exec chef — and has evolved into a customer favorite. Tipi Tapa is a municipality in Nicaragua, Central America — we named the preparation after the place because of the cocoa. This is the dish I always tell my customers is my favorite. I'm fond of saying that it's "a flavor explosion" of fruitiness, nuttiness, spicy curry, fish . . . it's amazing.

CURRIED CARROT PURÉE

6		large carrots
3	cups	potatoes, cooked (yukon gold or any kind)
2	tablespoons	curry powder, preferably Madras
2	tablespoons	unsalted butter
½	cup	whole milk
2	tablespoons	honey
		salt and pepper to taste

MANGO PURÉE

2		mangos, cleaned and chopped (can substitute frozen mango pieces)
1		shallot, minced
1	cup	water
½	cup	granulated sugar
½	cup	rice vinegar
1	teaspoon	kosher salt
¼	teaspoon	freshly ground black pepper

MACADAMIA OIL

1	cup	macadamia nuts, toasted in oven
1½	cups	canola oil
1	teaspoon	kosher salt
½	teaspoon	freshly ground black pepper

COCOA SPICE MIXTURE

¾	cup	cocoa powder
⅓	cup	chili powder
2	teaspoons	black pepper
⅛	cup	kosher salt
⅓	cup	brown sugar

SEA BASS

2½	pounds	sea bass, cut into 6 portions
2	tablespoons	canola oil
		salt and pepper to taste

1. Make the carrot purée. Peel, chop, and boil the carrots in salted water until very tender (approximately 35 minutes). Strain the carrots out of the water and put them in a food processor with the remaining ingredients. Purée the mixture until smooth (about 5 minutes), season with salt and pepper, and check for sweetness. Adjust the seasoning accordingly and keep warm until service.

CONTINUED >

2. Make the mango purée. Combine all the ingredients in a small sauce pot over moderate heat. Bring to a boil, lower to a simmer, and cook for 5 minutes. Place the mixture in a blender and purée until smooth. If it's too thick, adjust with water or add vinegar if it's too sweet. Reserve for service.

3. Preheat oven to 450°F.

4. Make the macadamia oil. Place all ingredients in a food processor and pulse 3 or 4 times until macadamia nuts break up and incorporate with the oil. (Be careful not to overprocess and make macadamia butter. Save that for another time when you're making fresh jelly or jam for a sandwich!)

5. Make the spice mixture. Place all ingredients in a small bowl and mix until combined.

6. Prepare the sea bass. In a large sauté pan, heat the oil on high heat. Put the spice mixture on a clean plate and dredge the skinless side of each piece of fish in the mixture. When the pan begins to smoke, add the dredged side down first and sear for about 30 seconds. Season with salt and pepper. Flip the piece over, and sear for another 30 seconds. Place the seared piece of fish on a baking sheet or in a baking dish. Sear the remaining fish. Put the baking dish in the oven for about 10 minutes, or until a toothpick can be pulled out cleanly from the fish.

7. To plate: Place the fish atop the curried carrot purée and top with 1 tablespoon of macadamia oil and 1 tablespoon of mango purée.

Colorful carrots from Crows Pass Farm in Temecula.

Karl Strauss Brewing Company

I n 2010, Karl Strauss Brewing Company celebrated the most important year in a beer drinker's life – the big 2-1. It was a true "coming of age" that marked 21 years of pioneering the craft beer movement in San Diego, California, which is now known as one of America's best beer cities. Located in Pacific Beach and currently distributed exclusively in Southern California, Karl Strauss ranks 40th on the list of Top Craft Breweries in the United States. The brewery is known for its best-selling Red Trolley Ale (a 2010 World Beer Cup Gold Medal winner), its Tower 10 IPA, and the innovative special-release beers it brews each year.

It all started back in the mid-1980s, when 2 beer-loving college grads set up shop in an apartment on Mission Beach, armed with newly minted degrees and an entrepreneurial spirit. Inspired by a brewpub they came upon while traveling through Australia, they wanted to open a microbrewery and reintroduce locally brewed beer to San Diego (an enterprise banned by Prohibition in the 1920s to early 1930s). As it happens, one of the founders was related to a man with a little brewing experience: Enter Karl (as in Karl M. Strauss, world-renowned master brewer). "Uncle Karl" consulted on the first 10-barrel brewery, developed the original beer recipes, and set up the initial quality-control practices.

After a year of writing IOUs to friends and family, overcoming archaic liquor laws, and tweaking the beer recipes, they were finally ready. On February 2, 1989, locals lined up around the block to try the first brewpub San Diego had seen in more than 50 years. Karl Strauss opened with just 3 beers: Karl Strauss Amber Lager (Karl's favorite), Gaslamp Gold Pilsner, and Downtown After Dark Brown Ale. For most people, it was the first time they had ever tasted freshly brewed beer.

A lot has changed since those early days. Karl Strauss Brewing Company now brews more than 30 different beers a year, including 6 core beers, 3 seasonals, and a host of special releases. Distribution has expanded to include more than 2,500 bars, restaurants, liquor stores, and grocery stores throughout Southern California. The original brewpub in downtown San Diego has grown to include 5 more brewery-restaurants throughout San Diego, Orange County, and Los Angeles. One thing that hasn't changed is the commitment instilled by "Uncle Karl" to brew fresh, quality beer every day. Karl's love of life, respect for others, and passion for handcrafted beer serves as the foundation for the company to this day.

Left to right: Fresh and locally brewed is the Karl Strauss way; Community Marketing Manager Ryan Ross; some of the brewery's star lineup.

SWEET POTATO–APPLE LATKES WITH LEMON VERBENA CRÈME FRAÎCHE

Yields 16 to 18 (3-inch) cakes • Total time: 24 to 48 hours / Active: 1 hour

I wanted to do something a little different for Passover — I had used sweet potato for a while, but my original twist had cinnamon crème instead of lemon verbena crème fraîche. When I added the apples to the sweet potato, it made the mixture wetter, so we had to tweak it a couple of times to get it just right. We have it now.

LEMON VERBENA CRÈME FRAÎCHE

1 to 2	tablespoons	cultured buttermilk
2	cups	heavy whipping cream
8	leaves	lemon verbena, chopped

LATKES

1		medium white or yellow onion
2	pounds	sweet potatoes or yams, peeled
1	pound	apples, peeled and cored (Granny Smith are great for their tanginess, but all varieties will work)
4		large eggs, slightly beaten
1	cup	all-purpose flour
2	tablespoons	salt
1	tablespoon	ground nutmeg
2	teaspoons	ground cinnamon
2	teaspoons	freshly ground black pepper
2	tablespoons	baking powder
		canola or vegetable oil (for frying)

APPLE-FENNEL RELISH (SUGGESTED SIDE DISH, NOT PICTURED)

1		shallot, minced
2	bulbs	fennel, minced
3		dried chipotles*
¼	cup	apple cider vinegar
2	cups	fresh apple juice
½	cup	brown sugar
6		Fuji apples, peeled, cored and finely diced
1	tablespoon	fresh lemon juice
1	tablespoon	fresh cilantro, chopped
		salt and pepper to taste

1. Make the crème fraîche. Combine the buttermilk, cream, and lemon verbena in a sauce pan and heat to tepid (not more than 85°F on an instant-read thermometer). Pour the warm cream into a clean glass jar, cover partially, and let it stand at room temperature (between 65°F to 75°F) for 8 to 24 hours, or until thickened. Stir and refrigerate at least 24 hours before using. The cream will keep for about 2 weeks in the refrigerator.

2. Make the latkes. Grate the onion, potato, and apple, and mix together well in a large bowl with the rest of the ingredients, except the oil.

CONTINUED >

Jewish Chef's Tip: The onions and potatoes will release liquid, and when combined with the egg, it makes for a soggy ball. So, strain the mixture to get rid of some of the unecessary liquid before forming.

3. For each potato pancake, take ¼ cup of mix and form it into a 3-inch circle on a cutting board. Continue with the rest of the mix until you have all pancakes formed. Cover the bottom of a skillet with ¼ inch of oil. Heat the pan until it is hot, but not yet smoking — about 375°F.

4. With a spatula, transfer the pancakes to the skillet and fry them until golden brown on one side, about 1 minute, then flip and continue cooking for another minute. Drain well on paper towels. Serve hot topped with crème fraîche and, if desired, the apple-fennel relish on the side.

Chef's Tip: Use 2 forks to flip the latkes.

5. Make the suggested apple-fennel relish side dish: In a sauce pot, sweat the shallot, fennel, and chipotles on low heat. Add the vinegar and reduce to almost dry. Add the apple juice, sugar, lemon juice, and apples and bring to a boil. Let simmer for about 10 minutes, then remove from heat. Add the cilantro, season with salt and pepper, and serve.

Austin and Ashleigh Gradillas at Raven Hill Orchard in Julian.

Above: Here I am having a look at the edible garden, with helpers (from left) Elina Wells, Katrina Lewis, and Dayton Harris.
Below: The third-graders' pizza oven.

Albert Einstein Academies

The garden project at Albert Einstein Academies in urban San Diego is truly a collective and community effort. Back in December 2007, the garden began when a team of parents, teachers, and students planted 45 fruit trees that had been donated by the Fruit Tree Planting Foundation. The following spring, parents and kids cleared shrubs and terraced a site for an edible garden. The students then created a worm bin and pledged their time to come with parents for regular weeding and watering duty.

Since 2008, the Einstein garden space has grown to include an herb garden, an Einstein Peace Garden (a community garden area and outdoor reading garden planted with fruit trees and native perennials), a children's garden (and castle topiary), a South African garden, a Moorish garden, a Japanese garden, a Pacific Island garden, and Baja gardens.

Today, under the direction of Terri Hughes-Oelrich, who organizes the garden committee, the kids at Einstein grow all sorts of heirloom and organic edible plants and herbs. Their delicious bounty includes salad greens, chard, broccoli, artichokes, tomatoes, kale, mustard greens, asparagus, onions, strawberries, blueberries, and grapes.

The garden also provides a starting point for lots of cool projects. The third graders, for example, planted wheat, ground it into flour, and made pizza in the wood-fired cob oven that they built. Terri says that one of the most gratifying aspects of being involved with the garden is "seeing the kids beg for carrots, onions, and swiss chard." Much of the garden's produce, she says with a grin, "never makes it out of the garden."

tree fruits

CALIFORNIA FARMS ARE HOME to a dazzling variety of tree fruits. In fact, almost every conceivable kind of tree fruit can be grown somewhere in the state. The great majority of California's tree fruit crop, however, comes in the form of citrus, stone, or pomaceous fruits — which are members of the order *Rosales* and are generally tree fruits with seeds or pits in the middle (and are also related to roses).

Citrus production in California is done on a staggering scale. More than 250,000 acres are dedicated to growing grapefruit, lemons, oranges, and tangerines. Navel and Valencia oranges make up the vast majority of that citrus (about 70 percent). The great output of citrus in the state is partly due to the fact that this fruit can be harvested in California year round. When the growing seasons of northern California are combined with those in the south, various kinds of lemons and grapefruits can be picked in every month. When the Navel orange crop (November to April) is combined with the Valencia crop (May to November), oranges of one kind or another are available year round.

California's primary *Rosales* (stone and pomaceous) fruit crops include apples, apricots, cherries, dates, figs, kiwi, peaches, pears, and plums. All together, these fruits are grown on more than 215,000 acres throughout the state — with the majority of acreage dedicated to peaches (about 30 percent) and plums (about 30 percent). Most of these delicious fruits are spring and summer bounties — they are harvested mostly from May through October.

In the kitchen, the uses for California tree fruits are basically unlimited. They can be used in all kinds of sweet or savory sauces, marinades, salsas, and chutneys, all of which can work well with fish, poultry, and meats of all types. These fruits also lend themselves extremely well to jarring and canning — jams, jellies, butters, dried, or candied.

Desserts, of course, are a whole other universe for fruits. If you've gotten your hands on some fresh apricots, apples, pears, cherries, plums, or peaches, there's probably nothing more satisfying than throwing together a tart, pie, cake, compote, or cobbler that features these naturally sweet and delicious ingredients.

ADOBO-GRILLED CHICKEN WITH APPLE-CHIPOTLE RELISH

Serves 6 to 8 • Total time: 24 to 48 hours / Active: 1½ hours

Adobo is found in countries all over the world, and it means different things in different cultures. In the Philippines, for example, adobo is a specific dish. In Mexico, it is a type of marinade made with chiles (like this recipe). With the apples, I think it's perfect for a summer-to-fall transition — and fall is a great time to grill.

ADOBO MARINADE

7		dried ancho or guajillo chiles*
12	cloves	fresh garlic, roasted
2	teaspoons	ground cumin
2	teaspoons	fresh oregano
1	tablespoon	kosher salt
½	teaspoon	ground cinnamon
⅓	cup	sherry vinegar or champagne vinegar
1		orange, zest and juice
1	cup	fresh cilantro, chopped
¼	cup	honey
¼	cup	canola or corn oil

CHICKEN

4	8- to10-ounce	boneless, skinless chicken breasts

APPLE-CHIPOTLE RELISH

1	tablespoon	canola oil
1		shallot, minced
3		dried chipotle peppers*
¼	cup	apple cider vinegar
2	cups	apple juice
½	cup	brown sugar
1	tablespoon	fresh lemon juice
6		apples of your choice (*not* Granny Smith), cored and finely diced
1	tablespoon	fresh cilantro, chopped
1	teaspoon	kosher salt
¼	teaspoon	freshly ground black pepper

1. Make the marinade. In a small sauce pot on high heat, combine the chiles and 3 cups of water. Once the liquid boils, turn it off and let it sit for 5 minutes. Strain the chiles, but reserve 1 cup of the liquid. Place the chiles, reserved liquid and all the remaining ingredients — except the oil — in a blender and process until smooth. While puréeing, slowly add the oil to emulsify. Coat the chicken breasts evenly on both sides with the marinade and refrigerate for at least 24 hours, but no longer than 48 hours.

2. Make the relish. In a medium sauce pot on low heat, add the oil and sweat the shallot and chipotles (that is, sauté until they give up some liquid and are translucent) for about 3 minutes. Add the vinegar and reduce the mixture to almost dry, about another 3 minutes. Add the apple juice, sugar, lemon juice, and apples, and bring to a boil. Take the mixture off the heat, add the cilantro, salt, and pepper. Reserve.

3. Grill the chicken pieces on a barbecue (or broil them in an oven if no grill is available) and top them with the relish to serve.

To Drink with Your Meal...

Wine: Smokiness, sweetness, spiciness, and fruit are the key notes in this dish, and they pair beautifully with **Gewürztraminer** or dry Rhone-style whites, such as a **Viognier**.
• Meridian Gewürztraminer
• Arrowood Viognier

Beer: A fruity and mild **English Bitter** or **IPA** will cut some heat while keeping the other flavors intact.
• Goose Island Honker's Ale
• Brew Dog Trans Atlantic IPA

SMOKED RIBEYE STEAK WITH BING CHERRY—HEIRLOOM TOMATO SAUCE

Serves 4 • Total time: 4 hours / Active: 40 minutes

This excellent combination of flavors was developed by one of my chefs early on — Reid Sinderud. He originally came up with the cherry-tomato sauce as part of a special, and it was so tasty we've used it ever since (more than a decade now). The fruitiness of the cherry goes really well with the smokiness of the steak, and the heirlooms highlight the sweetness of farm-fresh San Diego tomatoes.

SMOKED RIBEYE STEAK

| 2 to 3 | pounds | prime rib |
| | | salt and pepper to taste |

BING CHERRY—HEIRLOOM TOMATO SAUCE

2	tablespoons	canola oil
1	tablespoon	fresh garlic, minced
2	cups	bing cherries, stemmed and pitted
2	cups	red heirloom tomatoes, 1-inch dice
½	cup	granulated sugar
¼	cup	rice vinegar
1	cup	water
¼	cup	fresh basil, chiffonade
¼	cup	Chambord liqueur
1½	teaspoons	kosher salt
1	teaspoon	freshly ground black pepper

1. Season the steak with salt and pepper, and then smoke the meat for about 3 hours at or below 150°F, according to the manufacturer's instructions for your smoker. *(Note: You can use 1 tablespoon of liquid smoke* if you don't have or want to use a smoker.)*

2. While the steak is smoking, make the tomato sauce. Add the canola oil to a medium sauce pot on medium heat. Saute the garlic for 30 seconds. Add the cherries and tomatoes and continue to sauté for another 2 minutes. Add the sugar, vinegar, and water, bring to a boil, then lower to simmer for another 15 minutes. Add the basil and Chambord and season with salt and pepper to finish. Reserve for service.

3. When the steak is smoked, let it rest until you're ready to finish cooking. Grill the steak to your desired doneness, and let it rest for about 2 to 3 minutes before slicing and serving, topped with the sauce.

CUNNINGHAM FARM CITRUS–SEARED AHI WITH AVOCADO-MANGO SALSA

Serves 6 • Total time: 24+ hours / Active: 45 minutes

Citrus from Cunningham Organic Farm is so good I was inspired to do a recipe that highlighted their fruits. The avocado-mango salsa, which originally went with a crab salad, was so tasty that I used it in a bunch of other applications. The marinade has Asian elements, but it's not the typical one used for sesame-seared tuna. The citrus gives the fish a tartness that balances well with the salsa.

CITRUS MARINADE

5	pounds	mixed citrus (I use mandarin oranges, Navel oranges, kumquats, tangerines)
1	teaspoon	sesame oil
1	teaspoon	fresh ginger, grated
1	teaspoon	fresh garlic, minced
1	stick	cinnamon
3		star anise
1	tablespoon	honey
1	8-ounce can	coconut milk
1	stalk	lemongrass
½	bunch	fresh cilantro, chopped

AVOCADO-MANGO SALSA

1		mango, finely diced
1		Roma tomato
1		medium Hass avocado, finely diced
¼	teaspoon	dry mustard
2	tablespoons	fresh lemon juice
3	tablespoons	granulated sugar
¼		medium red onion, minced
½	teaspoon	kosher salt
¼	teaspoon	freshly ground black pepper

AHI

2	pounds	sashimi-grade ahi
2	tablespoons	sesame or grapeseed oil
		salt and pepper to taste

1. Make the marinade. Juice all of the citrus. In a small sauce pot on medium, heat the oil with the ginger, garlic, cinnamon, and star anise for about 1 minute. Add all the remaining ingredients — except the cilantro — and bring to a boil. Turn the heat down to low and simmer for about 30 minutes. Take it off the heat and add the chopped cilantro. When the liquid has cooled, put the ahi in the marinade and marinate in the refrigerator for no more than 24 hours.

2. Make the salsa. Cut tomato in half and make tomato petals. *(See Chef's Tip, Page 72)* Put all the ingredients in a bowl and mix until combined. Reserve for service.

3. Cook the ahi. Season with salt and pepper, and sear it on all sides in a hot sauté pan with the oil for about 30 seconds per side. Slice the fish and serve with the salsa.

4. Another option: Fry wonton pieces into chips and top each one with a piece of the ahi and some salsa.

To Drink with Your Meal...

Wine: The citrus components of this dish, mixed with the meatiness of the tuna, make it a good choice for **Chardonnay**. If you prefer to pair wines that accent more of the fruitiness, a full-bodied **Viognier** would also work nicely.
• Ramey Chardonnay
• Echelon Viognier

Beer: A citrusy **American IPA** will refresh the palate while providing the perfect complement to the range of citrus flavors in this dish.
• Ballast Point Sculpin
• Alpine Nelson

Cunningham's beautiful property on a misty day.

Cunningham Organic Farm

W hile we were at Cunningham, only the occasional hum of a distant helicopter from Camp Pendleton interrupted the peace and quiet of this beautiful place. Located in a gorgeous, secluded valley next to the Cleveland National Forest, the farm is nothing short of a lush, fruit-lover's paradise.

George and Gale Cunningham moved to DeLuz Canyon, north of Fallbrook, in 1974. With little experience and a lot of determination, they set out to become farmers. They knew next to nothing about the conventional methods of farming that used chemicals and pesticides, so the Cunninghams decided to "go natural" and grow organically. (This was before terms like *organic, sustainable,* and other "eco-friendly" concepts were commonly used.) Lucky for them, organic farming also produces the best-tasting, most nutritious, earth-friendly food possible.

As their experience with organic farming increased, George discovered that improving the soil was the most important work on the farm. He began by enriching his earth with by-products of the farm itself. He took algae and other water plants from the ponds on the property, and green waste from the compost pile, and tilled it back into the soil. He even "harvested" silt from the streams that run through the farm and used that to enhance and improve the earth. As George likes to say, all these practices are "part of a necessary and valuable process of chemical-free soil enrichment."

The Cunninghams have more than 60 acres in DeLuz, spotted primarily with citrus and avocados. A cherimoya grove provides a lush green backdrop to the lower pond, and persimmon trees line the paths to the adobe farmhouse. George is a fruit connoisseur – he can vividly describe the different tastes going on in each of his seven varieties of tangerines. He also happily chats endlessly about one of his personal favorites, the "cocktail fruit" tree, which is a cross between a pomelo and a tangerine.

The Cunninghams have come to embrace the special challenges of growing all kinds of interesting tropical fruit varieties in the semitropical climate of DeLuz. They strive, in particular, to grow fruit that most others do not. Among their unique crops are three types of guavas, meiwa kumquats, loquats, and even bananas.

More information about Cunningham Organic Farm is in Featured Organic Farms on page 202.

Above: Gale shows me the delicious flesh of an orange. Below (left to right): Buddha's Hand citron; George gives me the citrus tour; a cherimoya still on the tree.

PORK TENDERLOIN WITH SMOKED APPLESAUCE AND CITRUS COUSCOUS

Serves 8 to 10 • Total time: 3½ hours / Active: 1 hour

Sometimes, a recipe just happens. We had a smoker going one day — for one of our summer "Barbecue and Blues" nights — and we decided to throw some different stuff under the hood. My sous chef at the time put some apples in and they were incredible. Apples go really well with pork, hence the two together.

SMOKED APPLESAUCE

3	pounds	apples (any variety)
3½	cups	water
½	cup	molasses
1	teaspoon	kosher salt
1	teaspoon	freshly ground black pepper

CITRUS COUSCOUS

2	tablespoons	fresh garlic, chopped
2	tablespoons	shallots, chopped
1	teaspoon	fresh ginger, chopped
¼	cup	canola oil
1	teaspoon	mustard seed (can omit if not available)
½	teaspoon	ground cloves
2	cups	Israeli couscous*
1½	cups	fresh orange juice
2	cups	water
1	tablespoon	kosher salt
1	teaspoon	freshly ground black pepper
1		lime, zest and juice
1		mandarin orange or tangerine, zest and juice
2	tablespoons	honey

PORK TENDERLOIN

5	pounds	pork tenderloin
		salt and pepper to taste
1	tablespoon	canola oil

1. Make the applesauce. Core the apples and cut into quarters. Follow the instructions for your smoker and smoke the apples at or around 150°F for at least 2 hours. *(Note: You can use 1 tablespoon of liquid smoke* if you don't have or want to use a smoker.)*

2. In a medium sauce pot on low heat, combine the smoked apples with the remaining ingredients and let the mixture simmer for 20 minutes. In a food processor, pulse the cooked apples twice — just to break them up a bit. Adjust salt if necessary. Reserve for service.

3. Make the couscous. In a large sauce pan on medium heat, sauté the garlic, shallots, and ginger in canola oil. Turn heat to low and add the mustard seed and cloves, stirring to combine. Add the couscous and toast it for about 1 minute while stirring. Add the rest of the ingredients and bring to a boil. Lower heat and simmer until liquid is almost gone.

4. Preheat oven to 375°F. Season all sides of the tenderloin with salt and pepper and sear in a hot sauté pan. Transfer the pork to a roasting pan and cook for about 20 to 25 minutes, or until the internal temperature reaches 145°F. Let the meat rest for about 5 minutes before slicing.

5. Serve the pork over the couscous, topped with the smoked applesauce.

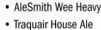

APPLE STRUDEL WITH RED WINE CARAMEL

Serves 6 • Total time: 2 hours / Active: 1½ hours

We were pressed for time to visit Raven Hill Orchard in Julian before all of the apples were gone. We arrived on a sunny, but windy October afternoon to gates that were perched open for my assistant Lisa, her 2 kids, and my book crew. Patrick, the owner, was waiting for us dressed like an artist with a top hat, a bright blue shirt, a pocket knife on his belt, and an Irish accent. When asked about his teepee on the property, Patrick told us that "it has given me a different perspective on my own relationship with the earth. It's a much more harmonious connection with my surroundings. It's my place of rest and rejuvenation." I remember buying a half gallon of freshly pressed apple juice that Patrick had made in an old machine for us — definitely the best $10 I ever spent on apple juice. The orchard has 7 varieties, including Gravenstein, ripening mid-August, to Golden Delicious, which are sweetest in late October. The apple orchard was planted 18 years ago to feed the growing need of the local pie companies.

STRUDEL FILLING

6		Granny Smith apples
2¼	cups	unsalted butter
¼	teaspoon	ground nutmeg
3½	cups	granulated sugar
1		orange, zest
2	tablespoons	ground cinnamon
1		package phyllo dough
½	cup	raisins (any kind is fine)
½	cup	pecans, toasted and chopped

RED WINE CARAMEL

3	cups	granulated sugar
1	cup	water
¼	cup	heavy whipping cream
½	cup	unsalted butter
2	cups	fruity red wine (non-oaky), reduced by half

1. Preheat oven to 450°F.

2. Peel, core, and slice the apples. Heat ¼ cup of the butter in a sauté pan and add the apples, nutmeg, ½ cup sugar, orange zest, and 1 tablespoon of the cinnamon. Continue cooking the apples on high heat until they are tender and show some nice caramelization. Remove from the heat and let cool.

3. Melt the remaining 2 cups of butter. In a bowl, combine the remaining 3 cups of sugar with 1 tablespoon of cinnamon. Unfold the phyllo dough on a clean work surface and cut it in half along the crease. Make a stack and put a damp cloth over the dough to keep it moist and pliable.

4. Take 2 sheets of dough, brush them all over with melted butter, cover the bottom half of each sheet with the apple mixture, and sprinkle some raisins and pecans on top. Sprinkle some cinnamon sugar on the entire sheet and then roll the dough from bottom to top while folding in the sides as you go. When the roll is complete, brush some butter on all sides to keep it moist. Set aside on a nongreased baking sheet and repeat the process until all of the apples are used.

5. Make the caramel. In a medium sauce pan over medium heat, combine the sugar and water. When the sugar turns a medium/dark amber color, take the mixture off the heat and slowly add the cream. Let the cream equalize the temperature and stop the boiling, then whisk in the remaining ingredients. Let the caramel stand for about 5 minutes to cool before service.

6. Place the rolls in the oven for 12 minutes, or until slightly browned. Cut into pieces and serve with the red wine caramel.

To Accompany Your Dessert...

Wine: The warm, comforting richness of this dessert calls for a rich, warming fortified wine, such as a **Tawny Port** or a **Port** made from a red wine.
- Orfila Tawny Port
- Hart Syrah Port

Beer: English **Barleywines** are terrific dessert beers with rich fruity and toffee flavors.
- Anchor Old Foghorn
- Samuel Smith's Barleywine

BANANA CRÈME BRÛLÉE

Serves 6 • Total time: 70 minutes / Active: 20 minutes

1	quart	heavy whipping cream
1		vanilla bean, split and scraped
½	teaspoon	pure vanilla extract
6		bananas
9		large egg yolks
¼	cup	granulated or raw sugar
¼	cup	raw or brown sugar (for caramelizing)

1. Preheat oven to 325°F.

2. In a medium sauce pot over medium heat, bring the cream, vanilla bean, and vanilla extract to a boil, stirring occasionally to avoid scorching.

3. Meanwhile, take 4 of the bananas, peel and dice them into 2-inch pieces. In a medium bowl, whisk together the egg yolks and the sugar. After the cream mixture has come to a boil, remove the vanilla bean. Then temper the eggs and sugar with the cream by slowly pouring the hot liquid into the eggs in a thin stream while continuously whisking (you want to avoid cooking the eggs). When all the cream is incorporated with the egg, pour the mixture into 6 (6-ounce) ramekins and evenly distribute the diced bananas in the ramekins. Place the ramekins into a large baking dish (or several smaller ones) and fill the baking dish(es) with warm tap water so it reaches about halfway up the sides of the ramekins. This is called a water bath. *(See Chef's Tip, Page 112.)*

4. Place the dishes in the oven and check them after 45 minutes. If you gently shake the ramekins and the mixture is set, they're done; take them out to cool. Allow the brûlées to come to room temperature before putting them in the refrigerator to finish chilling. Once completely chilled, sprinkle the tops with sugar, and burn them under a broiler or with a small kitchen torch. (If you don't burn the sugar, then it is called pot de crème). *Note: Don't caramelize the crèmes brûlées and then put them back in the refrigerator; the sugar will dissolve and come to the surface because of the humidity and condensation from refrigeration.*

5. The remaining 2 bananas can be sliced, sprinkled with sugar, and caramelized with a torch to place on top of the crèmes brûlées for garnish and additional flavor.

CITRUS MARSHMALLOWS

Serves 6 to 8 • Total time: 9 hours / Active: 30 minutes

When I have a spare minute (which is not often) I will flip through food magazines, just to look for interesting ingredients or techniques. I saw something similar to this — and I've always wanted to do marshmallows — especially for a kid's cooking class. The citrus component makes them unique, and you can use almost any kind, including lemon, lime, or grapefruit. And don't be afraid of the candy thermometer — it's not a big deal.

		butter (for greasing the pan)
		powdered sugar (for dusting)
¾	cup	water
3	tablespoons	unflavored gelatin (3 packets)
2	cups	granulated sugar
½	cup	evaporated milk
1		large orange, zest
1	teaspoon	pure vanilla extract
		orange decorating sugar*

1. Butter the bottom and sides of an 8- x 8-inch straight-sided baking pan. Dust liberally with sifted powdered sugar and set aside.

2. Pour ½ cup water into the bowl of a stand mixer fitted with the whisk attachment. Sprinkle the gelatin over the water and allow the gelatin to soften, about 10 minutes.

3. In a 3-quart sauce pan, combine the sugar, evaporated milk, and the remaining ¼ cup water. Stir over low heat until the sugar has dissolved. Bring the mixture to a simmer and cook, without stirring, until a candy thermometer registers 240°F, about 10 to 12 minutes. Pour the syrup into the gelatin mixture and beat it at low speed until incorporated. Increase the speed to high and beat until thick, fluffy, and tripled in volume, about 10 to 12 minutes. Beat in the orange zest and vanilla extract until just combined. Using a spatula, scrape the mixture into the prepared pan, smooth the surface, and sprinkle with orange decorating sugar.

4. Allow the mixture to set, uncovered, in a cool place (not refrigerated) for at least 8 hours or overnight. Remove the large marshmallow square from the pan and place it on a powdered sugar–dusted surface. Using scissors dusted with powdered sugar, cut the marshmallows into about 1-inch squares. Dip the cut sides into powdered sugar to prevent sticking. Store in an airtight container for up to 2 weeks.

To Accompany Your Dessert...

Wine: It's something of a challenge to pair marshmallows with wine, so this pairing may be for those looking for adventure. Given the sweetness and lightness of this dessert, a light and bubbly sweet wine, such as a **Sparkling Moscato** or, for a bit heavier choice, a **Muscat Port**, would likely do the trick.
• Bonny Doon Moscato
• South Coast Sweet Maggie Muscat Port

Beer: Don't be scared, there is a beer for every food. Highlight the citrus and counter the sweetness with a crisp Belgian **Wit** or tart Berliner **Weiss.**
• Ommegang Witte
• Dogfish Head Festina Peche

berries

BERRIES ARE ONE OF NATURE'S BEST CHARACTER BUILDERS; they remind us about the rewards of patience and hard work. A perfect, ripe, and full-flavored berry is a taste treat that has few equals — chefs as well as home cooks everywhere are always searching for the perfect batch. But great berries do not come easy. They are delicate things, often hidden from view on leafy bushes or vines. Most need to be picked by hand — each one individually — and at just the right time. Once picked, they must be handled with care and eaten relatively soon.

Californians are lucky when it comes to berries. Not only does almost every kind of berry grow in California, but the growing season is significantly longer than other berry-producing regions. The most common berry crops are strawberries, raspberries, blackberries, huckleberries, cranberries, gooseberries, currants, and barberries. (Blueberry cultivation recently has taken off as well.)

California's biggest berry crop is strawberries — the state produces about 90 percent of America's strawberries (an average of 1.8 billion pounds per year).

Grapes are also included in the berry family. They are classified as true berries because the fruit wall *(pericarp)* is fleshy all the way through. Modern grape crops in California have all been derived from two main species, the European *Vitis vinifera* — which provides varietals for many types of wine, as well as eating grapes such as Thompson Seedless (Sultana) and Red Flame Seedless. The American species, *Vitis lambrusca*, provides the common jam and juice grapes, such as Concord.

In the kitchen, fresh, ripe berries are incredibly versatile ingredients. They can be used in both sweet and savory ways, and can be used cooked or fresh. The sweetness of most berries makes them a natural focus of many kinds of desserts, from tarts and pies to sorbets and cobblers. In savory dishes, many berries — such as currants, gooseberries, or cranberries — provide a sweet and tart component that adds a special dimension to sauces and compotes.

When selecting berries, look for lightly firm fruit that still holds its shape. Most berries do not do well under the weight of large containers, and most will start molding if stored in warm temperatures or in containers without some air.

ROAST DUCK WITH CRANBERRY–GOAT CHEESE BREAD PUDDING

Serves 6 to 8 • Total time: 5 hours / Active: 1½ hours

When I put this on my menu, I was amazed. I've never gotten so many compliments about a duck dish. I think the beauty of it is that the duck gets crispy and has intense flavor, but it's not dry. And the bread pudding, Oy!

CRANBERRY–GOAT CHEESE BREAD PUDDING

1	quart	heavy whipping cream
1	quart	whole milk
2	sprigs	fresh thyme
1	sprig	fresh rosemary
12		large egg yolks
4	quarts	bread, chopped (any kind is fine — some types I like: rosemary, cranberry, apricot, date-walnut)
4	ounces	goat cheese
2	tablespoons	fresh thyme, chopped
1	cup	dried cranberries
⅓	cup	caramelized onions (*See Jeff's Kitchen Advice, Page 19*)
⅓	cup	pecans, chopped
		salt and pepper to taste

DUCK

3		whole ducks, cut in half with backbones removed and reserved (*See Chef's Tip, Page 110*)
1	cup	carrot, chopped
1	cup	onion, chopped (any kind is fine)
1	cup	celery, chopped
12	cloves	fresh garlic, chopped
2	gallons	water
2	teaspoons	kosher salt
2	teaspoons	freshly ground black pepper
½	cup	dried cranberries
¼	cup	fresh rosemary, chopped
2	sprigs	fresh thyme

1. Make the bread pudding. Preheat oven to 350°F. In a medium sauce pot on medium-low heat, heat the cream and milk with thyme and rosemary to almost boiling. In a medium bowl, whisk the egg yolks while slowly adding the cream mixture to temper the eggs (don't do it too fast or the eggs will cook). Strain the egg mixture into a clean container. Put the bread into the bowl and mix with the strained liquid. Add the goat cheese, cranberries, chopped thyme, caramelized onions, and pecans and season with salt and pepper. Pour into a greased baking dish, cover with aluminum foil, and bake for 30 minutes. Remove foil and cook for 15 more minutes. Cut into pieces and reserve for service.

2. Prepare the ducks. Preheat oven to 350°F. Place the backbones and ½ cup carrot, ½ cup onion, and ½ cup celery on a baking sheet and roast for about 30 minutes. Place the roasted ingredients, along with 6 garlic cloves and 2 gallons of water in a stock pot and bring to a boil. Lower the heat and simmer for 3 hours.

3. Strain the duck stock and reduce on medium-high heat for about 1 hour, or until it has thickened to a sauce consistency. Season with salt and pepper, add cranberries, and reserve for service.

4. Meanwhile, poke the ducks repeatedly with a fork and season both sides with salt and pepper. Line a baking dish with the remaining rosemary, thyme, remaining garlic and vegetables. Lay the ducks on top and bake in the oven for about 3 hours, or until the ducks are crispy and you can twist the leg bone.

5. To plate: Place a piece of bread pudding on a plate along with the duck and top with the sauce.

To Drink with Your Meal...

Wine: This is a wonderfully rich and hearty dish that begs for a rich, full-bodied red, such as an old-vine **Zinfandel** or a **Syrah**.
- Seghesio Old Vine Zinfandel
- Fallbrook 33° North Syrah

Beer: A sweet **Red Ale** will contrast with the savory elements, while a hoppy **American Red** will complement the fresh herbs.
- Karl Strauss Red Trolley Ale
- Green Flash Hop Head Red

RASPBERRY-MARINATED CHICKEN STIX WITH MINT VINAIGRETTE

Serves 4 to 6 (as an appetizer) • Total time: 24 + hours / Active: 1 hour

This simple recipe is perfect for picnics. I first developed it for Memorial Day and Labor Day cookouts, but you can serve the cooked chicken almost any way — hot, warm, or at room temperature. I pair it with mint vinaigrette because lots of people do basil and cilantro, and I like to use another flavor. I've been meaning to try the marinade with duck and pork — it would probably be great.

RASPBERRY MARINADE

2	cups	raspberries, crushed
½	cup	water
¼	cup	olive oil
¼	cup	fresh cilantro, chopped
1	tablespoon	fresh mint, chopped
1	tablespoon	fresh garlic, minced
1	tablespoon	fresh lime juice

CHICKEN

1	pound	boneless, skinless chicken breasts, cut into strips

MINT VINAIGRETTE

3	cups	fresh mint
1	cup	rice wine vinegar
¼	cup	granulated sugar
1	teaspoon	kosher salt
1	teaspoon	black pepper
1	teaspoon	fresh ginger, grated

1. Combine all the marinade ingredients in a medium bowl, add chicken strips, and marinate for up to 24 hours.

2. Make the mint vinaigrette. Combine all the ingredients in a blender and purée until smooth.

3. Before cooking the chicken, soak 4 to 6 wooden skewers in water for at least 30 minutes. Skewer the marinated chicken securely.

4. Grill the chicken skewers.

5. To plate: serve the skewers with a drizzle of the mint vinaigrette.

To Drink with Your Meal...

Wine: The sweet and savory mix in this light dish is a nice match for a medium-bodied white that has both a fruity character and a nice acidity, such as a **Pinot Gris** or a **Sauvignon Blanc**.
- Beringer Pinot Gris
- Frog's Leap Sauvignon Blanc

Beer: A **Belgian IPA** or **Pale** with a good fruity character and medium hops bitterness would be a great match with this dish.
- Gouden Carolus Hopsinjoor
- North Coast Pranqster

To Accompany Your Dessert...

Wine: There are few wine and food pairings that can beat Stilton cheese and a nice **Port**. The berry component in this dessert would also make it a wonderful match for an exotic, blueberry-tinged **Aleatico**, which is tougher to find but well worth the effort.
• Orfila Tawny Port
• Hart Aleatico

Beer: A **Double/Imperial IPA** with a tropical and citrus character will highlight the floral and fruity flavors of the Stilton.
• Alpine Pure Hoppiness
• Bells Hopslam

STILTON CHEESECAKE WITH PLUM-BLUEBERRY COMPOTE

Serves 8 to 12 • Total time: 1½ hours / Active: 45 minutes

I first made this dessert in 2003, for a specialty catering job. It was for a small group of people in Alpine, California, and they were all really into wine. Before that dinner, I had tried the cheesecake with goat cheese, which was nice and tart, but I thought it would be extra cool to put a blue-veined cheese in there. Anyone who's into wine knows that a Stilton or a bleu is a match made in heaven for all types of dessert wines — whites, reds, ports, sauternes — anything.

CRUST

¾	cup	unsalted butter, melted
1	cup	graham cracker crumbs
2	cups	hazelnuts, toasted and finely chopped

FILLING

2	pounds	cream cheese, softened
1	cup	sour cream
2	cups	granulated sugar
2		large eggs
2	tablespoons	pure vanilla extract
1		lime, juiced
12	ounces	stilton cheese (or other blue cheese)
3	tablespoons	unsalted butter

PLUM-BLUEBERRY COMPOTE

12		fresh plums, pitted and diced
3	cups	blueberries (or 4 small packages)
1	teaspoon	ground ginger
½	teaspoon	ground cloves
1	teaspoon	ground cinnamon
1	tablespoon	fresh lime juice
1	tablespoon	fresh orange juice
¼	cup	fresh basil, chiffonade
1	tablespoon	water
1	tablespoon	cornstarch
1	tablespoon	granulated sugar (if needed)

1. Make the crust. Mix the melted butter, graham cracker crumbs, and hazelnuts to form the crust.

2. Preheat oven to 300°F.

3. Make the filling. In an electric mixer with the whip attachment, combine the cream cheese, sour cream, and sugar and whip for about 5 minutes until light and airy. Add the eggs one at a time until incorporated, then the vanilla, lime juice, and stilton cheese, but don't break up the cheese.

CONTINUED >

4. With the 3 tablespoons of butter, grease a 10-inch spring form pan and firmly pack the crust into the bottom. Pour the cream cheese mixture into the pan and bake for about 45 minutes, or until set (you can also make small, individual cheesecakes in small spring forms, but you will have to adjust the cooking time accordingly).

5. Make the compote. In a medium sauce pot, combine all the ingredients except the basil, water, and cornstarch. Bring to a boil, reduce heat, and simmer for about 5 minutes. Add the basil.

6. In a small bowl combine the water and cornstarch to make a slurry. Add the slurry to the sauce pot while simmering and stir to thicken. Remove the compote from the heat. Check for sweetness. If the plums aren't ripe enough, you may need to add the sugar.

7. To plate: Top each serving of the cheesecake with a tablespoon of plum-blueberry mixture.

Blue Heron Farm

As soon as you arrive at Blue Heron Farm, you can't help being awestruck by the beauty of the property. Lush, green, rolling hills. Neatly trenched furrows in the deep brown soil. Tall, elegant old trees. It definitely feels like the "Garden of Eden," as owner Andrea Peterson likes to call it.

Andrea is also great at making everyone who comes to visit feel welcome. (The farm is also a wonderful bed & breakfast.) Before our personal tour, we had a nice cup of coffee.

Blue Heron Farm is tucked into the hills of Fallbrook, California, just six miles inland from the ocean. Unlike many other farms in the region that must adapt to a wild mix of microclimates, Blue Heron is essentially frost free. That means Andrea is picking her mangos, guavas, and many other kinds of delicious tropical fruit all year long!

It was clear to Andrea as soon as she arrived on the property in 1979 that she would farm the land organically and with the greatest respect for its natural beauty. She started out by growing subtropical fruit trees, but by 1985, she was ready to begin what she called her "small experiment" — growing baby lettuce for the emerging baby vegetable market. Well, that "small experiment" evolved into a business that eventually sent hundreds of pounds of lettuce overnight to New York City restaurants every day, and all year round. At that point, Peterson Specialty Produce lettuces had become featured items on the menus of many of Manhattan's most famous dining destinations.

The recent awareness about organic farming has fueled a hugely increased demand for local organic produce. This surge in demand has been wonderful for Blue Heron Farm, as well as many other local growers. (Today, Andrea can sell a great deal of Blue Heron's fruits and vegetables within miles of the property, which makes her very happy.) Blue Heron produce is available in San Diego and Los Angeles, mostly at Farmers' Markets and in restaurants and upscale grocery stores.

Of course, you can always sample the farm's bounty by visiting the secluded B&B in Fallbrook.

As a guest, you can enjoy the beauty and tranquility of the farm, pick and taste whatever you want, and partake of the farm's daily harvest at the breakfast table.

More information about Blue Heron Farm is in Featured Organic Farms on page 202.

Left to right: Sweet, ripe strawberries; Andrea shows me the property; sugar snaps soak up the sun; some of the baby veggies that put Blue Heron on the map.

To Accompany Your Dessert...

Wine: Because Muscat is used in the making of this dish, a **Sparkling Moscato** or still **Muscat** are the natural accompaniments. If you prefer a weightier dessert wine, a **Tawny Port** would also work nicely.

- Orfila Muscat Canelli
- South Coast Black Jack Port

Beer: To highlight the chocolate, think **Baltic** or **Imperial Porter**. For something unique, try a sweeter **Belgian Kriek**.

- Stone 09.09.09
- Lindeman's Kriek

CHOCOLATE CREPES WITH ORFILA MUSCAT–MACERATED STRAWBERRIES

Serves 8 • Total time: 4 to 5 hours / Active: 2 hours

This recipe is actually a world premiere: I developed it for this book and during the creation of this book. The idea struck me while I was tasting the dessert wines at Orfila. We had been talking about wanting another dessert recipe, and one that featured strawberries. I loved the Orfila Muscat so much, that I wanted to make it the focal point of the dish — how great is that?

MACERATED STRAWBERRIES

8		large strawberries
2	tablespoons	granulated sugar
1¼	cups	Orfila Muscat Canelli*
1	tablespoon	fresh lemon juice
2	tablespoons	unsalted butter (for heating sauce)

CHOCOLATE CREPE BATTER

1½	cups	all-purpose flour
½	cup	cocoa powder
6	tablespoons	powdered sugar
1	teaspoon	kosher salt
2	tablespoons	canola oil
2	cups	whole milk
2		large eggs
½	teaspoon	pure vanilla extract
		vegetable oil (as needed)

MUSCAT REDUCTION

1	cup	Orfila Muscat Canelli*

STRAWBERRY CREAM FILLING

1	pound	cream cheese, at room temperature
½	cup	sour cream
½	cup	powdered sugar
2	tablespoons	pure vanilla extract
12		strawberries, quartered
		cocoa nibs* (for garnish)

1. Macerate the strawberries. Slice the strawberries and put them into a medium bowl. Add the remaining ingredients except butter, and refrigerate for at least 2 hours.

2. Make the crepe batter. Sift together the flour, cocoa powder, sugar, and salt in a large bowl. In a medium bowl, combine the oil, milk, eggs, and vanilla and whisk until blended. Add the liquid mixture to the dry mixture slowly, whisking to dissolve any lumps. Refrigerate for about 1 hour.

3. Make the muscat reduction. Put the wine into a small sauce pot over medium high heat and bring to a boil. Lower the heat to maintain a rolling boil and continue boiling until liquid is reduced to about ⅛ cup. Remove from heat, cool, and reserve for service.

CONTINUED >

4. Make the strawberry cream filling. In the bowl of an electric mixer with the paddle attachment, beat the cream cheese until smooth. Add the sour cream, sugar, and vanilla and continue beating for another minute or so (scraping down the sides of the bowl as necessary). Put the mixture into a large bowl and fold in the quartered strawberries.

5. Cook the crepes in a crepe pan (lightly oiled with vegetable oil, then wiped clean). Set the crepes aside until all are done.

6. Lay the crepes on a clean work surface and put about ¼ cup of the filling in the center of each crepe, leaving room at the bottom and around the edges. Fold the bottom of the crepe over the filling and gently roll up. Continue this process until all of the crepes are filled.

7. At this point, the crepes can be eaten cold – just top them with the macerated strawberries and the Muscat reduction and cocoa nibs. If you prefer warm crepes, then you'll need to place them on a platter and refrigerate them for 1 hour first. In a large pan over low heat, melt the butter, add the macerated strawberries, and warm the sauce. Add 8 of the assembled crepes to the pan and cook for 1 minute, basting with the strawberry sauce. Remove the crepes from the pan, set aside, keep warm, and continue with the remaining crepes.

8. To plate: Line up 2 to 3 crepes, top with some macerated strawberry sauce, and then drizzle the Muscat reduction. Garnish with cocoa nibs.

Strawberries at Be Wise Ranch in Escondido.

Left to right: Farm Manager Leonard Vargas gives me the tour; gorgeous, just-picked organic vegetables; students work the fields in early spring.

San Pasqual Academy

When you visit the campus of San Pasqual Academy, it's obvious that they have taken the idea of a school garden to a whole new level. They're not growing vegetables on a tiny plot or fenced-in yard, they're farming more than 8 acres!

The academy was created in 2001 as a unique collaboration between the County of San Diego and various private agencies. Today, it is home to about 140 foster teens, their house parents, alumni, and elders who volunteer as surrogate grandparents. The school, which is a national model for preparing foster youth for life after foster care, was also the first in the nation to be created for that purpose. "Our focus is to take teens who are not in stable settings and get them ready to be out in the world on their own," says Yvonne Campbell, the director of special projects.

One of San Pasqual's most recent successes is their student-run agriculture program. Under the direction of Farm Manager Leonard Vargas, 15 to 20 students take responsibility for nearly all aspects of growing food. As participants, the teens learn not only about how food is grown and harvested, but also how it is sold. Dragon Organics (named for the school mascot) is the produce business the students created. "The students have been charged with determining how they will be paid and how to make a distinction between those who plant, harvest, and sell the produce," Yvonne explains. "This also gives them a real-life experience of what it's like to run your own business."

Dragon Organics grows a wide variety of fruits and vegetables, including lettuces, lemons, mandarins, grapefruits, strawberries, cabbage, carrots, broccoli, beets, and swiss chard. Their produce can be found at a number of San Diego's top restaurants, including The Lodge at Torrey Pines, The Marine Room, and Stone Bistro. They have also launched a CSA (community supported agriculture) program and have begun selling at the Farmers' Market in Scripps Ranch.

Clearly, the academy is doing something right. While the national high school graduation average for teens in foster care is 60 percent, for the past 5 years 94 percent of San Pasqual's senior class has graduated from high school, and 73 percent went on to college.

STRAWBERRY EMPANADAS

Serves 8 to 10 • Total time: 2½ hours / Active: 2 hours

I love using empanada dough for a whole bunch of things. It works for savory dishes as well as sweet ones, and this dough recipe came from my former sous chef Benito's Mexican grandmother. I hadn't made a strawberry dessert with empanada dough before this book project, but I've become quite fond of this recipe.

LEMON CURD

5		large egg yolks
1	cup	granulated sugar
4		lemons, zest and juice
4	tablespoons	butter, chilled and cut into little pieces

EMPANADAS

4	cups	all-purpose flour
¼	cup + 1 tablespoon	granulated sugar
1½	teaspoons	baking powder
1	tablespoon	kosher salt
⅔	cup	shortening, at room temperature
⅔	cup	ice water
7		medium strawberries, cut into ½-inch dice
1	teaspoon	fresh lemon juice
1	tablespoon	fresh basil, chopped
2		large eggs, whisked with a little water (for egg wash)
		cocoa nibs* (for garnish)

1. Make the lemon curd. Add enough water to a medium sauce pan to come about 1 inch up the side and bring to a simmer over medium-high heat. Meanwhile, combine the egg yolks and sugar in a medium metal bowl and whisk until smooth, about 1 minute. Measure the lemon juice and — if needed — add enough cold water to reach ⅓ cup. Add the juice and zest to the egg mixture and whisk thoroughly.

2. Place the metal bowl with the lemon mixture over the simmering water. The metal bowl should be large enough to fit on top without touching the water — this is very important, so the eggs don't cook too fast and scramble. Whisk the egg mixture continuously until the mixture is thickened and coats the back of a spoon (approximately 8 minutes). Remove from the heat and stir in the butter a little at a time. Once all the butter is melted in, transfer the curd to a clean container and cover by placing plastic wrap directly on the surface of the curd (this prevents a "skin" from forming). Allow the curd to cool completely before serving. Refrigerate for up to 2 weeks.

3. Preheat oven to 350°F.

4. Make the empanadas. In a medium bowl, sift together the flour, ¼ cup of the sugar, baking powder, and salt. Cut the shortening into the flour as though you were making a pie crust by working it in with your fingertips until the mixture resembles coarse crumbs. Sprinkle the dough with just enough ice water to allow the mixture to just hold together. Knead briefly and allow the dough to rest covered for about 10 minutes. Roll the dough out on a lightly floured board to about ⅛-inch thick. With a 4½-inch ring mold, cut rounds out of the dough and set aside. Ball the remaining dough up again and again, keep rolling it out and cutting rounds.

5. In a small bowl, combine the strawberries, 1 tablespoon of the sugar, lemon juice, and basil. Set aside.

6. On a clean work surface brush each round with the egg wash. Place 1 tablespoon of the strawberry mix in the middle of each round and fold the dough over. Fasten the edges together by pressing with a fork. Bake the assembled empanadas on a baking sheet until golden brown (approximately 15 minutes).

7. To plate: Arrange 2 or 3 empanadas on a plate and garnish with lemon curd and cocoa nibs.

To Accompany Your Dessert...

Wine: Sweetness and lemony tang are what this wonderful dessert is all about. For a light accompaniment, try a Muscat or a late-harvest **Riesling** or **Gewürztraminer**. For something with a bit more body and spice, try a late-harvest **Zinfandel**.

- Bonny Doon Vin de Glaciere
- South Coast Late Harvest – Old Vine Zinfandel

Beer: Embrace the fruity and citrus flavors with a true Bavarian **Hefeweizen**. Add a splash of orange juice for a **Hefemosa**.

- Weihenstephaner Hefeweissbier
- Hacker-Pschorr Hefeweissbier

cocktails

here are some of my favorites —
so get your drinks on!

BUDDHA'S HAND LEMON-BASIL MARTINI

Yields: 2 (750-milliliter) bottles • Total time: 4+ days / Active: 20 minutes

This citrus concoction was inspired by the incredible Buddha's Hand citrons that grow at Cunningham Organic Farm. These lemony fruits only have a little juice, but they have lots of oil in their skin, which makes them great for infusions.

LEMON-BASIL-INFUSED VODKA

2	cups	fresh basil, chopped
2		Buddha's Hand citrons, zest
4	tablespoons	granulated sugar
2	750-milliliter bottles	vodka

MARTINI

¼	ounce	simple syrup (See Chef's Tip, Below)
2½	ounces	infused vodka
¼	ounce	sweet 'n' sour (See Chef's Tip, Below)

1. Place all the lemon-basil-infused vodka ingredients into a medium sauce pot and heat to approximately 100°F. Remove from heat and let the liquid come to room temperature. Put the entire mix into an airtight bottle and let it sit for a minimum of 4 days. Strain before using and drink away!

2. Place all the lemon-basil martini ingredients into a cocktail shaker with ice, shake, and strain into a martini glass. Garnish with fresh basil and a float of thinly sliced lemon or a lemon twist.

Chef's Tips: Simple Syrup and Sweet 'n' Sour:

1. Simple syrup can be made by heating equal parts sugar and water to dissolve the sugar. Anything can be added to change the flavor profile (lemongrass, ginger, lime or orange zest, cinnamon, cloves, rosemary, basil, etc.)

2. My sweet 'n' sour recipe at Terra is equal parts lemon juice, lime juice, simple syrup, and water.

STRAWBERRY-MANGO SANGRIA

Serves 8 • Total time: 1 to 2 days / Active: 30 minutes

Everyone does red sangria, so here's a way to be different: white sangria. And instead of using the usual peaches or oranges, I switch it up and use local strawberries and even local mangos (when they're available).

1		mango, peeled and pitted
6		strawberries
¼	cup	simple syrup
		(See Chef's Tip, Page 189)
6	ounces	fresh orange juice
6	ounces	fresh lemon juice
2	sticks	cinnamon
1	750-milliliter bottle	viognier wine
8		strawberries, sliced
		(for garnish)
1		mango, peeled, pitted
		and sliced (for garnish)
1	liter	lemon-lime soda
8	sprigs	fresh mint (for garnish)
1		orange, sliced (for garnish)

1. Place the first 5 ingredients in a blender and purée until smooth. In a large glass container, combine the puréed mixture with the cinnamon sticks and the viognier. Cover and refrigerate for at least 24 hours and up to 48 hours.

2. When ready to serve, pour the sangria into an ice-filled pitcher about two-thirds full. Add the fresh fruits, top with lemon-lime soda, and stir gently to mix. Serve in wine glasses with ice, mint, and fresh fruit.

CRANBERRY-ORANGE STAR ANISE VODKA

Yields 2 (750-milliliter) bottles • Total time: 4+ days / Active: 15 minutes

Simple story: We created this drink after Thanksgiving, when we had too many cranberries around. We had been in the vodka-infusion mode for a while, so we used a bunch of cranberries and added two flavors that pair really well: anise and orange.

1	pound	fresh cranberries
2	cups	fresh orange juice
8		medium oranges, zest
¼	cup	star anise
2	750-milliliter bottles	vodka

1. In a medium sauce pot, mix together the cranberries, orange juice, orange zest, and star anise and bring to a boil. Reduce heat and let simmer for 3 to 4 minutes. Take the mixture off the heat and mix with the 2 bottles of vodka. Put the entire mix into an airtight container and let it sit for a minimum of 4 days. Strain and drink away!

STRAWBERRY CAIPIRINHA

Serves 1 • Total time: 10 minutes / Active: 10 minutes

This popular Brazilian drink is the South American cousin of the mojito. The cane liquor is muddled with fresh lime and mint and then served on ice, but here I added fresh strawberries to the mix.

1		lime, cut into quarters
2	teaspoons	granulated sugar
4		strawberries
2½	ounces	cachaça* (Brazilian cane liquor; can substitute rum)
	splash	soda water strawberries (for garnish) mint leaves (for garnish)

1. Muddle 3 wedges of the lime, the sugar, and 3 strawberries in a rocks glass. Add ice, cachaça, soda water, and serve. Garnish with sliced strawberries, lime wedge, and mint. Yum!

BLUEBERRY MOJITO

Serves 1 • Total time: 10 minutes / Active: 10 minutes

Mojitos are classic Cuban drinks — traditionally made with rum. Tuesday night is Mojito night at the restaurant, and we're always trying to be creative. Sooner or later, if it's a tasty fruit you can throw into a glass, there's a good chance it will become a mojito at Terra!

1		lime, cut into quarters
15		fresh blueberries
1¼	ounces	blueberry vodka
	splash	soda water
1	tablespoon	simple syrup

(See Chef's Tip, Page 189)

1. Muddle half of the lime and 10 blueberries together in a rocks glass. Add ice, vodka, and simple syrup, then the soda water, and serve. Garnish with the remaining blueberries and a lime wedge. That's livin' large!

APPLE PIE MARTINI

Yields 2 (750-milliliter) bottles • Total time: 4+ days / Active: 20 minutes

I had a bunch of Hachiya persimmons that came in a shipment, and I wanted to use persimmon in an infusion. The Hachiyas are usually soft and overripe (only good for jellies and jams), so I found some Fuyu persimmons, which work great when you cook them.

PERSIMMON-CINNAMON-INFUSED VODKA

2	pounds	Hachiya or Fuyu persimmons, 1-inch dice
2	sticks	cinnamon
2	750-milliliter bottles	vodka

APPLE PIE MARTINI

½	ounce	persimmon vodka
1¼	ounces	apple vodka
½	ounce	vanilla vodka
½	ounce	half and half crushed graham crackers (for glass rim)

1. Place all persimmon-cinnamon-infused vodka ingredients into a medium sauce pot and heat to about 100°F. Remove from heat and let the liquid come to room temperature. Put the entire mixture into an airtight bottle and let it sit for a minimum of 4 days. Strain before drinking and enjoy!

2. Place all the apple pie martini ingredients into a cocktail shaker with ice and strain into a chilled martini glass. Wipe the rim of the glass with water (along the edge) and dust the rim with graham cracker crumbs. Put a cinnamon stick through a slice of apple or persimmon as a garnish.

changing the world one fork at a time

WHILE CONTEMPLATING THE WORK THAT'S GONE INTO THIS BOOK — and the work left to do after the book is finished — I began to get a headache: it was a migraine, actually. When I first got interested in the idea of promoting local, sustainable, and organic food, my initial focus was on local farms and school gardens. But the more I got into it, the more work I realized needed to be done. It seems I had opened up the proverbial "can of worms" along the way. While working with Central Elementary's advisory board here in San Diego, I found there were a bunch of big organizations, such as Slow Food, International Rescue Committee, and San Diego County Childhood Obesity Initiative — as well as many concerned citizens, chefs, restaurateurs (myself included), parents, schools, and government agencies — that were very involved in farm-to-school, obesity, and hunger issues all around the world. This is a big movement — and it's getting bigger. Seventeen million kids live in food-insecure households and NOW is the time to make a difference.

Every day that's gone by since has been a learning process for me. Each time I visit a school garden or a farm I learn more about our food system and more about the people trying to lay the groundwork for a better tomorrow. I now realize that most of us don't know where our food comes from anymore. It seems as though we have a "generational gap of ignorance" toward food. Part of this is simply the era in which we live. In my lifetime, vast rural areas have been eaten up by developments, which has drastically reduced the number of farms and farmers. Dual-income households have become the norm, and — with the quickened pace of family life — prepared and fast foods have gained in popularity.

THE CHILDHOOD OBESITY PROBLEM

The topic of childhood obesity is now at the forefront of many conversations across the country, even for First Lady Michelle Obama. The Childhood Obesity Initiative reports a startling statistic: More than 1 in 4 children in San Diego County is either overweight or obese. This number is staggering to me. As a chef, I feel a responsibility to make it better. Many of my fellow chefs share my concern. Chefs all over the world have begun working to support more sustainable local food systems and to promote the idea of a food chain that goes "from farm to fork." Cheryl Moder, the director of the Childhood Obesity Initiative, puts it this way: "The process by which food travels from farm to fork may not seem like an important part in the solution to childhood obesity, but it is. Our food system has great potential to improve the economic, environmental, and general health of a community. A healthy food system slows down the process from farm to fork and invites communities to better understand the foods they eat and those who grow them. It provides an opportunity for families and children to ask questions about their food, to touch it, smell it, taste it, and build connections that help establish life-long healthy habits." Cheryl made me realize that we need to revisit our methods of farming, rebuild agriculture, and really take a look at the nutrition standards our government has adopted for our kids.

Fortunately, San Diego is blessed with many great farms and farmers that are in the process of working toward a centralized "food hub" and information system that will get locally grown products into schools and other institutions more frequently. I am working with Jonathan Reinbold from the Tierra Miguel Foundation who is heading up the Farm to Institution part of a $16 million grant that was given to the County of San Diego by the Centers for Disease Control and Prevention. I also meet regularly with the Childhood Obesity Initiative to coordinate our efforts. Through them, we work on policy and environmental strategies that help make the healthy choice the easy choice in all places where families and children live, work, play, worship, and learn. This includes the school food environment or "lunch room." Currently, this is where my greatest passion lies.

THE SHAME OF THE SCHOOL LUNCH

I think I can now honestly call myself a "food activist" with an emphasis on school food. I've been involved with school gardens for a few years, and I had the pleasure of being asked to participate in a Whole Foods–sponsored event at Albert Einstein Academies. The school won a national competition, and the prize was a personal visit from Chef Ann Cooper, known to many as the "Renegade Lunch Lady." The event was the culmination of 12 chefs who were challenged to come up with a breakfast or lunch dish that the kids would try and judge, all for under $1. Yes, it was done. (Items such as Beef and Quinoa Soup with Grilled Cheese, and Chicken-Broccoli Calzones with Mozzarella and Marinara were big hits.) I had been following Chef Ann on Twitter, and I contacted her prior to her visit. I was able to get her into Terra for a private dinner the night after the event. It was great to talk with her and to see her passion. She really inspired me to help "fix" the system (yes, I want to be the man who leads the "food revolution" that will work for your kids). Ann said that she runs her district's lunch program like a restaurant: and the key is filling the seats. (Just as in any restaurant, if you can't get butts in seats, then you're losing money.) A school cafeteria is basically a restaurant — the labor is the same, the rent is the same, the electricity is on, and you need as many diners as possible. Well, in the school system they call this the "participation rate;" it's the number of kids who eat the school lunch. Traditionally, some food service directors, in order to get a higher participation rate, serve the unhealthy but popular foods such as french fries, pizza, burgers, mac 'n' cheese — I think you get the idea. There are many chefs, myself and Chef Ann included, who want to make those options healthier but still just as appealing. And the cost of doing that will drop as participation rates rise. What's more, it's proven that kids get better grades when they eat better meals.

For a number of years, I've been working with Gary Petil, food services director for the San Diego Unified School District and also a longtime friend. Together, we've organized school-wide festivals celebrating the harvest and showcasing school gardens. With his permission, I was able to work with Central Elementary School's principal and garden coordinator to harvest baby greens, carrots, and herbs from their garden. I then proceeded to work with a few fifth-grade students to clean and process the produce in their own cafeteria before putting it all out in their own salad bar. WOW! There was nothing more gratifying than seeing the pride in kids' faces — getting the high-fives and hugs — when the other students found out the salad bar was filled with produce from the garden at Central Elementary.

Recently, I had the pleasure of seeing Jan Poppendieck give a talk about her new book *Free for All: Fixing School Food in America*. It was riveting. As she puts it, "Our spectacular failure to provide fresh, appealing, healthy meals for all our children is the result of a series of specific and identifiable social choices that we have made: a massive disinvestment in our public schools, an industrialized food system, an agriculture policy centered on subsidies for large-scale commodity production rather than a public health approach to school food programs." Jan is not the only one addressing this issue. I learn more and more each day about the National School Lunch Program and how agribusiness has influenced lunch choices and policy, cash and commodity reimbursements, and the ridiculous marketing dollars that dictate and sway what can be served to our children. It's shameful, but true: our kids are eating what "big business" wants them to eat.

When children from low-income families qualify for free or reduced-price lunches, the government reimburses schools for each meal served. Today, that rate is about $2.70, but only about $1 of that is allocated for the actual food. The rest goes to labor and other expenses charged to food service. Commodity reimbursements include products purchased by the government as a form of agriculture subsidy (corn-based products, for example) that are then provided to the schools for free. In addition to the federally reimbursable lunches, there is another category of food served at schools that "compete" and have no rules governing their nutrition. These are the "junk" options that have high appeal to the kids, but little nutritional value. There are many advocates fighting to remove competitive items and make the reimbursable lunches healthier. This whole system is being evaluated and will hopefully be improved with the Child Nutrition Reauthorization Bill, which was recently up for renewal.

One of the biggest problems facing school lunch programs is that most of the kitchens are lacking the equipment necessary to prepare healthy, cooked-from-scratch meals. A great many kitchens lack the skilled labor to process fresh local fruits and vegetables, even if they were given access to them. Here in San Diego, I am working with a group of local chefs who are consulting with the school districts and are providing the instruction and support to launch a program that will train school kitchen personnel in the handling and processing of fresh produce. Currently, we are piloting programs with different school districts, working with their food services teams, and evaluating skill levels, equipment, and processes in their kitchens. We spend time reinventing recipes and menu protocols and conducting training sessions to make recommendations in order to implement our farm-to-school initiative. We work with foundations and the nonprofit sector to get donations for uniforms, kitchen utensils, and equipment. We also do a good deal of work setting up the networks that enable locally sourced fruits and vegetables to get easily from the farms to the schools. The goal is to get the kitchens to make as much from scratch as possible and to eliminate the unhealthy, processed garbage they have been serving up to our kids.

A TRANSFORMATION ON THE WAY

The recent growth in organizations dedicated to improving food systems and addressing the root causes of obesity is very encouraging. It means the message is getting out, and it means that communities all over are beginning to rethink what food should be. When a community begins to truly value the food it eats, a transformation begins to take place. Programs like community gardens, school gardens, Farmers' Markets, and farm-to-institution programs start to flourish — and this helps to drive down the cost of healthy foods by creating thriving food environments.

The profiles in this book highlight some of the inspiring work taking place throughout Southern California to shape a healthy future and a healthy food system. These are some of the programs and organizations that will make childhood obesity, poor nutrition, and diets full of highly processed foods a thing of the past. Whether it's teaching children to grow their first tomato, shopping at a Farmers' Market, or partnering with schools to make programs like farm-to-school a reality, everyone has a role to play in creating a healthy community. The transformation will take time, but — with the continued commitment of individuals and organizations like those highlighted in this book — real, substantial change is on the horizon.

Please make a difference. Get involved!

Tierra Miguel Farm

I was totally stoked about finally having a chance to meet the folks at Tierra Miguel in person. I have been working with them for years and have long admired their dedication to the organic movement, as well as their involvement in bringing the important issues of food system advocacy to Southern Californians.

We pulled into the farm — which is nestled in a beautiful mountain valley about 45 minutes north of San Diego, at the base of Palomar Mountain — and were met by Mil Krecu, the farm's manager. It wasn't long before we were wheelin' all over their 85 gorgeous acres!

Mil explained that the farm's location has a distinct microclimate, which means crops need to be chosen carefully. It gets pretty cold in the winter (it's at the foot of one of the area's biggest mountains), and that seems to be good for growing a whole bunch of stone fruit, such as plums, apricots, peaches, nectarines, cherries, and persimmons. On other parts of the property, you can find orchards of apples, mulberries, pecans, and walnuts.

"One of the primary goals of Tierra Miguel is to engage in socially responsible agriculture," Jonathan Reinbold, the farm's director, later told me. He explained that Tierra Miguel is not only certified organic, but is also "biodynamic." Biodynamic farming is an enhanced organic technique that involves managing a farm with a holistic approach that encourages biodiversity and living soil.

It was clear while visiting that Tierra Miguel is about much more than just farming and selling produce. Everyone here is focused on promoting the viability of sustainable agriculture through educational programs and community food projects.

Most of the fresh fruits and vegetables from Tierra Miguel are distributed throughout Southern California through a community supported agriculture (CSA) program. Unlike "industrially produced food" the CSA creates a direct relationship between consumers and producers. CSA members buy a share of the farm prior to a season, and assume the risks and benefits associated with small-scale agriculture. Jonathan says that they view their CSA "not as a method to purchase food, but rather as an investment in farmland preservation and one's local economy that supplies the investor with a weekly or biweekly return of the farm's production."

More information about Tierra Miguel Farm is in Featured Organic Farms on page 202.

Left to right: Seedlings, a beet fresh from the ground, and chatting with Farm Manager Mil Krecu in a field of cauliflower.

At Central Elementary, we eat fresh salsa made with tomatoes and cilantro right out of the school garden.
From left: Esmeralda Lam, Melina Ramirez, me, Diana Moreno, and Agustin Lozano.

Food Activism and Other Resources

California Avocado Commission
www.avocado.org
Features growers, industry information, recipes, avocado facts, and history.

Chef Ann Cooper
www.chefann.com, www.foodfamilyfarming.org
Ann Cooper — chef, author, and educator — advocates better food for all children. She founded the Food Family Farming Foundation to focus on solutions to the school food crisis. Its pivotal project is The Lunch Box web portal that provides free tools, recipes, and connections to support school food reform.

Chez Panisse Foundation
www.chezpanissefoundation.org/
In 1996, Chef Alice Waters established the Chez Panisse Foundation. It envisions a school curriculum and school lunch program where growing, cooking, and sharing food at the table gives students the knowledge and values to build a humane and sustainable future.

Childhood Overweight and Obesity Prevention Initiative
www.surgeongeneral.gov/obesityprevention/
Today, 12.5 million American children are overweight — more than 17 percent. Overweight children are at greater risk for many serious health problems. This initiative, sponsored by the United States surgeon general, promotes the importance of healthy eating and physical activity at a young age to help prevent overweight and obesity. Working together, we can ensure our children's health — and their future.

Child Nutrition Reauthorization Bill
www.schoolnutrition.org/
Every 5 years the window of opportunity opens on Capitol Hill as lawmakers and their staffs work together to improve and reauthorize federal Child Nutrition Programs. During this time a bevy of questions are asked: What works well? What isn't working? How can we address new needs? For school nutrition professionals, the Child Nutrition Reauthorization Bill brings a special responsibility to answer these questions in order to ensure quality, healthy, safe meals are provided to children every school day.

Edible San Diego

www.ediblecommunities.com/sandiego/

This magazine and website celebrate those who work to bring us the freshest quality food: farmers, ranchers, and growers committed to creating healthier and more sustainable methods of working with plants, animals, and the land, as well as wineries, brewpubs, coffee roasters, and food artisans.

Jamie Oliver's Food Revolution

www.jamieoliver.com/campaigns/jamies-food-revolution

This food revolution is about saving America's health by changing the way you eat. It's not just a TV show, it's a movement for you, your family, and your community. Educate yourself about food and cooking. Find out what your child is eating at school. Make only a few small changes and magical things will happen. Switching from processed to fresh food will not only make you feel better but it will add years to your life.

Lets Move! "Chefs Move to Schools" Program

www.letsmove.gov

In spring 2010 schools interested in using local chefs as a resource for their cafeterias and nutrition programs may sign up for the "Chefs Move to Schools" program created by First Lady Michelle Obama. The First Lady launched the "Chefs Move to Schools" program to encourage chefs across the country to get involved in their communities by volunteering their skills in local school cafeterias. The program, run through the U.S. Department of Agriculture, calls on America's chefs to adopt a local school and work with teachers, parents, school nutritionists, and administrators to help educate kids about food and nutrition. Administrators or principals of K–12 schools and chefs who want to volunteer are invited to sign up online at www. letsmove.gov to get connected with each other.

Local Harvest

localharvest.org

This site features a directory of Farmers' Markets, family farms, and other sources of sustainably grown food in your area and where you can buy produce and grass-fed meats, and where you can find restaurants and other food businesses that support organic, local, and sustainable farming.

National School Lunch Program

www.fns.usda.gov/cnd/lunch/

The National School Lunch Program is a federally assisted meal program operating in public and nonprofit private schools and residential child care institutions. It provides nutritionally balanced, low-cost or free lunches to children each school day.

San Diego Childhood Obesity Initiative

http://ourcommunityourkids.org/

The San Diego County Childhood Obesity Initiative is a public/private partnership whose mission is to reduce and prevent childhood obesity in the county by creating healthy environments for all children and families through advocacy, education, policy development, and environmental change. The initiative creates, supports, and mobilizes partners from various sectors to provide leadership in the prevention and reduction of childhood obesity.

San Diego Roots

www.sandiegoroots.org

This sustainable food project is dedicated to educating, cultivating, and empowering sustainable food communities in San Diego County. Its website lists events, programs, and where to find locally grown food, including organic markets, Farmers' Markets, CSAs, farmstands, community gardens, sustainable seafood, and San Diego restaurants that use locally grown food.

Slow Food

slowfoodusa.org

This national organization supports, good, clean, and fair food. Its website features links to upcoming events, latest news, food education, information about joining, and finding slow food in your area.

Slow Food San Diego (SFSD)

www.slowfoodsandiego.org

Slow Food San Diego supports community efforts toward a greater understanding and availability of quality, sustainable, and local food. SFSD partners with the area's artisanal food producers, regional growers, chefs, and like-minded individuals and community organizations to promote the culture of good, clean, and fair food. SFSD is committed to preserving food traditions and reviving the table as a center of family and community.

Slow Food Urban San Diego

www.slowfoodurbansandiego.org

Slow Food Urban San Diego seeks to create dramatic and lasting change in the local food system. Its mission is to reconnect urban San Diegans with each other, rediscover food traditions and cultural heritage, and educate its community about the plants, animals, fertile soils, and waters that produce its food. In addition, it supports the mission, tenets, programs and values of Slow Food USA. It also seeks to inspire a transformation in food policy, production practices, and market forces so that they ensure equity, sustainability, and pleasure in the food people eat.

Tierra Miguel Foundation

www.tierramiguelfarm.org

The foundation is dedicated to exploring the potential for setting up a socially responsible community that can work together for agricultural renewal and sustainable farming practices. It provides education and supports local programs, including the Farm to Institution part of a $16 million grant that was given to the County of San Diego by the Centers for Disease Control and Prevention.

The Victory Garden, PBS Television Series

www.pbs.org/wgbh/victorygarden/

Information, instructions, recipes, and lots of video clips for anyone who wants to grow their own fruits and vegetables are available on this program and on the pbs website.

Victory Gardens San Diego

www.victorygardenssandiego.com

Working hand-in-hand with several San Diego food-movement groups, Victory Gardens San Diego encourages and assists in the development of sustainable, healthy, Earth-friendly home, community, and school food gardens throughout the San Diego area.

Featured Organic Farms

With Patrick Brady of Raven Hill Orchard

1. Be Wise Ranch
www.bewiseranch.com
20505 San Pasqual Road, Escondido, CA 92025
(760) 746-6006
bewiseranchcsa@gmail.com

2. Blue Heron Farm
www.blueheronfarmbandb.com/farm/index.htm
5910 Camino Baja Cerro, Fallbrook, CA 92028
(760) 643-0092
andreahp3@sbcglobal.net

3. Crows Pass Farm
www.crowspassfarm.com
39615 Berenda Road, Temecula, CA 92591
(951) 676-8099

4. Cunningham Organic Farm
www.cunninghamorganicfarm.com
P.O. Box 1522, Fallbrook, CA 92028
(760) 728-7456
cunninghamorganicfarm@gmail.com

5. Raven Hill Orchard
1284 Julian Orchards Drive, Julian, CA 92036
(760) 765-2431

6. Sage Mountain Farm
www.sagemountainfarm.com
40630 Sage Road, Aguanga, CA 92544
(951) 767-1016
phil@sagemountainfarm.com

7. Stehly Farms Organics
www.stehlyfarmsorganics.com
32542 Aquaduct Road, Bonsall, CA 92003
(760) 731-6517
info@stehlyfarmsorganics.com

8. Sun Grown Organics
www.sungrownorganics.com
(800) 995-7776
info@sungrownorganics.com

9. Suzie's Farm
www.suziesfarm.com
1856 Saturn Boulevard, San Diego, CA 92154
(619) 662-1780
CSA info: rodrigo@suziesfarm.com
Local chefs: robin@suziesfarm.com
Farmers' Market info: britta@suziesfarm.com

10. Tierra Miguel Farm
www.tierramiguelfarm.org
14910 Pauma Valley Drive, P.O. Box 1065
Pauma Valley, CA 92061
(760) 742-4213

Featured Wineries & Brewery

1. Orfila Vineyards and Winery
www.orfila.com
13455 San Pasqual Road
Escondido, CA 92025
(800) 868-9463

2. South Coast Winery Resort & Spa
www.southcoastwinery.com
34843 Rancho California Road
Temecula, CA 92591
(866) 994-6379

3. Fallbrook Winery
www.fallbrookwinery.com
2554 Via Rancheros
Fallbrook, CA 92028
(760) 728-0156

4. Hart Family Winery
www.hartfamilywinery.com
41300 Avenida Biona
Temecula, CA 92591
(951) 676-6300

5. Milagro Farm Vineyards
and Winery
www.milagrovineyards.com
Ramona, CA 92065
(858) 456-9463

Karl Strauss Brewing Company (Main Brewery)
www.karlstrauss.com
5985 Santa Fe Street, San Diego, CA 92109
(858) 273-2739

Product Resource Guide

Page 21: Phyllo dough. Available locally at Ralphs and Vons grocery stores (in frozen food section). Online at www.amazon.com.

Page 28: Annatto seed. Available locally at Ralphs grocery stores, and Thuan Phat Supermarket, 6935 Linda Vista Road, San Diego, CA 92111, (858) 505-0168. Online at Mexgrocer, www.mexgrocer.com, (877) 463-9476; and Penzeys Spices, www.penzeys.com, (800) 741-7787.

Page 28: Achiote paste. Available locally at Thuan Phat Supermarket, 6935 Linda Vista Road, San Diego, CA 92111, (858) 505-0168. Online at Mexgrocer, www.mexgrocer.com, (877) 463-9476, and at www.amazon.com.

Page 28, 56, 96: Round gyoza/potsticker wrappers. Available locally at Ralphs grocery stores, and 99 Ranch Market, 7330 Clairemont Mesa Boulevard, San Diego, CA 92111, (858) 974-8899, www.99ranch.com. Oonline at Phil-Am Food, www.philamfood.com, (201) 963-0455.

Page 33: Lemon avocado oil. Available locally at Whole Foods Markets. Online at Made in California, www.madeincalifornia.net, (866) 479-8934.

Pages 37, 82: Chipotle chiles with adobo sauce. Available locally at Ralphs grocery stores. Online at Mexgrocer, www.mexgrocer.com, (877) 463-9476.

Page 37: Slider buns. Available locally at Bread & Cie, (619) 683-9322, www.breadandciecatering.com; Ralphs grocery stores carry Sara Lee Soft & Smooth Mini Buns; Trader Joe's carries mini hamburger buns as well as delicious brioche bread that work great for sliders.

Page 43: Wasabi powder. Available locally at Ralphs grocery stores. Online at www.amazon.com.

Page 60: Frozen banana leaves. Available locally at 99 Ranch Market, 7330 Clairemont Mesa Boulevard, San Diego, CA 92111, (858) 974-8899, www.99ranch.com. Online at Gourmet Sleuth, www.gourmetsleuth.com, (408) 354-8281.

Pages 85, 117: Truffle oil. Available locally at Whole Foods Markets, and Great News!, Pacific Plaza, 1788 Garnet Avenue, San Diego, CA 92109, (888) 478-2433, www.great-news.com. Online at www.amazon.com.

Page 85: Dandelion vinegar. Available online at Swiss Chalet Fine Foods, (800) 347-9477, www.scff.com. (Note: You must search website with keywords "vinegar dandelion." If you search for "dandelion vinegar" you will be unsuccessful.)

Page 105: Dried heirloom beans. Available locally at Whole Foods Markets. Online at Purcell Mountain Farms, (208) 267-0627, www.purcellmountainfarms.com.

Page 105: Veal demi-glace. Available locally at Whole Foods Markets and Great News!, Pacific Plaza, 1788 Garnet Avenue, San Diego, CA 92109, (888) 478-2433, www.great-news.com. Online at Club Sauce, www.clubsauce.com, (888) 560-3562.

Pages 106, 158: Liquid smoke. Available locally at Ralphs grocery stores (in barbecue sauce aisle). Online at www.amazon.com.

Page 117: Pickled ginger. Available locally at Whole Foods Markets and Ralphs grocery stores. Online at www.amazon.com.

Page 142: Agave sweetener. Available locally at Trader Joe's, and Ralphs grocery stores (in the sugar/baking aisle). Online at www.amazon.com.

Page 145: Mirin (sweet cooking rice wine). Available locally at Whole Foods Markets and Ralphs grocery stores. Online at www.amazon.com.

Page 157: Dried ancho or guajillo chiles. Available online at Mexgrocer, www.mexgrocer.com, (877) 463-9476.

Page 151, 157: Dried chipotle peppers. Available online at Mexgrocer, www.mexgrocer.com, (877) 463-9476.

Page 164: Israeli couscous. Available locally at Trader Joe's. Online at www.amazon.com.

Page 171: Orange decorating sugar. Available locally at Ralphs grocery stores. Online at www.amazon.com.

Page 182: Orfila Muscat Canelli. Available locally and online at Orfila Vineyards and Winery, 13455 San Pasqual Road, Escondido, CA 92025, (800) 868-9463, www.orfila.com.

Page 182, 187: Cocoa nibs. Available locally at Great News!, Pacific Plaza, 1788 Garnet Avenue, San Diego, CA 92109, (888) 478-2433, www.great-news.com. Online at Swiss Chalet Fine Foods, (800) 347-9477, www.scff.com.

Page 192: Cachaça (Brazilian cane liquor). Available locally at BevMo!, www.bevmo.com. Online at Wally's, (310) 475-0606, www.wallywine.com.

ADDITIONAL RESOURCES

Bristol Farms, 8510 Genessee Avenue, San Diego, CA 92122, (858) 558-4180, www.bristolfarms.com (fresh produce, meats, stocks, sauces, cookware)

Chef's Resource, (866) 765-2433, www.chefsresource.com (chef tools, kitchenware, gourmet goods)

The Chefs' Warehouse, (718) 842-8700 extension #20104, www.chefswarehouse.com (specialty products, gourmet goods)

D'Artagnan, Inc., (800) 327-8246, www.dartagnan.com (poultry, meats, sausages, stocks, sauces)

Dean & Deluca, (800) 221-7714, www.deandeluca.com (chef tools, kitchenware, meat, seafood, wine, gourmet goods)

More than Gourmet, (800) 860-9385, www.morethangourmet.com (sauces and stocks)

Trader Joe's, check your local store or www.traderjoes.com (high-quality, natural ingredients, seasonal products)

Whole Foods Market, check your local store or www.wholefoodsmarket.com (natural and organic products)

Williams-Sonoma, (877) 812-6235, www.williams-sonoma.com (chef tools, kitchenware, tools, gourmet goods)

Recipe Index

The colors of fall at Raven Hill Orchard in Julian.

Luscious fruit at Cunningham Organic Farm north of Fallbrook.

Index

One of the many types of garlic grown at Sage Mountain Farm in Aguanga.